Hidden Treasures
of the Hudson Valley

Anthony P. Musso

Hidden Treasures
of the Hudson Valley

Anthony P. Musso

Copyright © 2018 by Anthony P. Musso

All rights reserved. No part of this publication may be reproduced, stored in or introduced into a retrieval system, or transmitted in any form, or by any means (electronic, mechanical, photocopying, recording, or otherwise), without the prior written permission of both the copyright owner and the publisher of this book.

ISBN 978-0-9886027-5-5

Manufactured in the United States of America

NetPublications, Inc

675 Dutchess Turnpike, Poughkeepsie, NY 12603

This book is dedicated to my granddaughter Isabella Anne. May you always believe in yourself, live your dreams to the fullest and remain curious about the world around you. Your fate in life is in your hands!

Table of Contents

Acknowledgments..8

Preface..9

1915 Erie Railroad Station (Chester)...............................11

Amawalk Friends Meeting House (Yorktown Heights)............15

Andries Dubois House (Wallkill)....................................19

Beth David Synagogue (Amenia)....................................23

Bodine's Tavern (Montgomery).......................................27

Bull Stone House (Campbell Hall) 31

Caramoor (Rosen Estate) (Kathonah)..............................35

Chrystie House (Beacon) 39

Chuang Yen Monastery (Carmel) 43

David Crawford House (Newburgh)..................................47

Derick Brinckerhoff Mansion (Fishkill) 51

Desmond Estate (Newburgh)..55

District #9 School House (Goshen) 59

Dubois-Kiersted House (Saugerties)................................63

Estherwood (Dobbs Ferry)...65

Fighting Quakers of Milton (Milton)................................69

First Columbia County Courthouse (Claverack) 73

Firthcliffe Firehouse (Cornwall) 77

Fish and Fur Club (Nelsonville) 79

General Hathorn Stone House (Warwick) 81

German Reformed Church Parsonage (Germantown).............85

Gilead Cemetery (Carmel)...89

Glebe House (Poughkeepsie)..93

Harmony Hall (Sloatsburg)...97

Hill-Hold Farmstead (Campbell Hall) 101

Horace Greeley House (Chappaqua) 105

Howland Library/Cultural Center (Beacon) 109

Indian Rock Schoolhouse (Amenia) 111

Innisfree Garden (Millbrook) 115

Jacob T. Walden House (Walden) 119

Jasper Cropsey House and Studio (Hastings-on-Hudson) 123

Jug Tavern (Ossining) 127

Leland Castle (New Rochelle) 131

Lewis Tompkins Hose (Beacon) 135

Moffat Library (Washingtonville) 139

Montgomery/Livingston House (Rhinebeck) 143

New Hamburg Train Tunnel (New Hamburg) 147

Old Drovers Inn (Dover Plains) 151

Old Southeast Church (Southeast) 155

Patriot's Park (Tarrytown) 159

Poets' Walk (Red Hook) 163

Potash House (Pleasant Valley) 167

Poughkeepsie Regatta (Poughkeepsie) 169

Quitman House (Rhinebeck) 173

Rest Haven (Monroe) 177

Skinny House (Mamaroneck) 181

Smith Tavern Complex (Armonk) 185

Standard House (Peekskill) 189

Stissing House (Pine Plains) 191

Stone House Intersection (Kingston) 195

Stoutenburgh Family Cemetery (Hyde Park) 199

Thomas Paine Cottage (New Rochelle) 203

Vassar Brothers Institute (Poughkeepsie) 207

Village of Bedford (Bedford) 211

Yelverton Inn (Chester) 215

Acknowledgments

It is with a deep sense of gratitude that the author wishes to acknowledge the following local historians and residents of communities throughout the Hudson Valley for their invaluable assistance in gathering information about many of the sites featured in this book:

Kathleen Alevras, Bedford Historical Society, Sophia Bernier, Jennifer Betsworth, John Bonafide, Roy Budnik, Chester Historical Society, Renee Fogarty, Cliff Foley, John Foreman, Michael Frazier, Friends of Harmony Hill, Friends of Hathorn House, Albert Gerney, Lawrence E. Gobrecht, Dr. Maung Htoo, Barbara Imbasciani, Alicia A. Jettner, Jug Tavern of Sparta, Inc., Nancy Kelly, Karen Morey Kennedy, William E. Krattinger, Robert D. Kuhn, Steven S. Levy, Ann Linden, The Masters School, Joan McAdam, Sr. M. Justin McKiernan, David Miller, Virginia Moore, Robert Murphy, Museum of Rhinebeck History, Austin O'Brien, Minisink Chapter of the NSDAR, Joanne Pagnotta, Clifton Patrick, Ruth Piwanka, Saugerties Historical Society, Tom Schroeder, Dr. Julie Seely, Peter Shaver, Willa Skinner, Charles W. Snell, Thomas Paine Cottage Museum, Stephen Tilly, Lynn Beebe Weaver, Geoff Welch.

Photographs by Anthony P. Musso
Book edited by Beth Quinn

Preface

New York's Hudson Valley region boasts an incredible number of sites that played an important role in laying the foundation for this nation's prosperity. It was home to numerous early settlements and was known for its critical participation in the American Revolution, as well as the ingenuity and innovation of its earliest citizens.

While a fair number of locales typically attract hundreds of thousands of visitors every year to tour Gilded Age mansions, presidential libraries and other mainstream tourist sites, many lesser known sites often go unnoticed despite their intriguing history.

In this, the third volume of the Hidden Treasures of the Hudson Valley series, the author identifies another fifty-five sites and shares their contributions to the fabric of our local and national history: former homes of leading citizens, Hudson River School artists and wealthy entrepreneurs; vintage schoolhouses where eight grade levels were taught by one teacher in a single room; and taverns and inns where some of our early politicians and military leaders met to strategize. These locations make ideal destinations for day trips and weekend getaways.

Read about a three-story house that's only ten feet wide, which was built using only scrap material during the nation's Great Depression. Visit an important train station, now a museum, where trains carrying passengers and freight once stopped on their way west for both business and leisure. And tour the mansion and take in a musical performance at the former estate of a wealthy international banker and attorney who willed the property to enhance the arts in the region.

Similar to the first two volumes in this series, each historical narrative outlined here concludes with either a physical address or, in the case of sites off the beaten path, exact driving directions to enable readers to easily visit the attraction. Because a vast number of "hidden treasures" are overseen and administered to by local municipalities, historical societies, or other volunteer groups, the majority of sites are very affordable.

Now sit back and visit more "hidden treasures of the Hudson Valley."

1915 Chester Railroad Station

On April 24, 1834, James Pierson, the owner and operator of several mines and mills in Ramapo, New York, Rockland County, persuaded the New York Legislature to authorize the construction of the New York and Erie Railroad. The line originated in Piermont, New York, and traveled north approximately four hundred miles to Dunkirk, on Lake Erie.

Because of the number of towns located along the route, the railroad enabled Pierson to greatly expand his marketplace and the distribution of his products.

While the railroad's construction moved forward without serious problems, when it reached the Village of Chester, Orange County, it had to contend with what local residents called "black dirt" – meadows that were basically huge swamps. Workers had to drive hundreds of piles fifty feet down into the wetland to reach solid ground for a base for the railroad. A trestle of equally strong lumber was then built to support the line.

In 1841, the first station to be built on the line was in Chester. It was an isolated structure in a landscape that primarily consisted of wilderness. The towns of Chester and Goshen became the first stations along the route to be assigned full-time agents. Thaddeus Selleck assumed the position in Chester and he arranged the first shipment of 240 quarts of milk to New York City.

Arnold, then in command at West Point. In exchange for money, he obtained the plans and troop numbers stationed there, so that the British could take the fort by force.

After benefiting from the hospitality of Underhill, Andre was captured later that day in Tarrytown. Other members of the Amawalk Friends were victims of numerous raids during the war that resulted in lost livestock and provisions; the British even confiscated some residents' property.

Good behavior within the group was strictly enforced. Minutes of the meeting's activity included dealing with the undesirable behavior of two male members, who – according to notes – were in the practice of "frolicking, such as dancing and wearing superfluous clothing."

Education was an extremely important concern for the Friends during that period and appropriate books, including the Holy Bible, the Journal of (Quaker founder) George Fox and Joseph Gough's History of the Quakers were purchased by subscription. The meeting was very supportive of the Nine Partners Boarding School that was established in 1896 in Millbrook, Dutchess County.

As the meeting continued to flourish, a larger timber meeting house forty feet long by thirty feet wide was proposed in 1784. By July 1787, the new house of worship was completed and paid for. For geographical reasons, the Amawalk Meeting became part of the Chappaqua Monthly Meeting but in 1798, it was designated a monthly meeting on its own and had the Peach Pond, Salem-Bedford, Peekskill and Croton meetings under its care.

In 1828, Quakers nationwide experienced a schism or split when a number of Friends decided to follow the more liberal teachings of traveling Long Island preacher Elias Hicks rather than those of Quaker founder George Fox. The Amawalk Friends in large part favored Hicks's teaching and – dubbed "Hicksites" – they retained the meeting house while orthodox Friends left to continue practicing the Fox principles.

Among the latter group was James Brown, the clerk (or overseer) of the Amawalk Meeting. Although Brown and a number of others left and rebuilt another meeting house (no longer standing) in Yorktown in 1832, he declined to give up the Book of Minutes and papers to the Hicksities remaining; a new book was purchased and a new clerk, Samuel Halstead, was appointed.

It was not until 1874 that the original titles and deeds of trust for property occupied by the Amawalk Meeting were returned to the Hicksites.

On Dec. 14, 1830, the now Hicksites meeting house was destroyed by fire, the second one to experience that fate. The meeting's members united with the resolve that a new one would be built. A committee was established to oversee its construction and the project was completed in August 1831 at a cost of $1,272.94.

By the mid-1830s the Amawalk Meeting – and the preparative meetings in its care – was thriving. Amawalk reported having thirty-five families, with Croton's ten, Salem's thirteen and Peekskill's sixteen, for a total of seventy-four in the community. By 1871, Amawalk boasted eighty families, Salem thirty-two, and Peekskill twenty. The Croton Meeting had been discontinued in 1848. But things would soon change.

Over time, failing to attract new members or even a strong attendance at Sunday worship, the preparative meetings were discontinued, with their members joining the Amawalk Friends Meeting. Friends became politically active, writing letters to the New York Legislature on a variety of issues.

They opposed and protested the manufacture and sale of alcohol in 1882, the lowering of the legal age of consent for young girls, from sixteen to thirteen years of age in 1891, and they urged life imprisonment rather than the death penalty for serious crimes in 1893.

With dwindling membership continuing, the Amawalk Meeting became an Executive Meeting in 1897, and six years later the meeting was incorporated. By 1938, due to the ever decreasing numbers of members, a decision was made to limit its meetings to summer months only.

During World War ll, the Friends made patchwork quilts and sent them overseas for those in need. In 1955, the Amawalk Friends sponsored two "Hiroshima Maidens," victims of the 1945 U.S. bombing who traveled to the United States for plastic surgery.

Dubois died in 1780, and the house passed down through his family. During the early- to mid-19th century, the house underwent extensive renovations, including the replacement of the original front entry with a recessed Greek Revival-style entrance, along with a number of interior Greek Revival-style components. The changes reflected both the preferred style of the era along with the ongoing prosperity of the Dubois clan.

The south side of the house is also built of brick. However, unlike the structure's front façade, which was brick laid in Flemish bond, the south side's bricks were laid in English bond. By contrast, the west side of the house was constructed of timber framing with brick noggin and clapboard over the original material.

The house's interior is laid out with a center hall stairway flanked by two parlors. Each parlor has a room behind it; the one on the south side is a kitchen. Several small bedrooms occupy the second floor.

The house was occupied by members of the Dubois family through the late 20th century. The Historical Society of Shawangunk and Gardiner acquired the house in 1998 and applied for and received a $7,500 New York State grant in 2003, which financed a historic structure report on the building.

Two excavations on the property uncovered artifacts that indicated the house was built on land formerly occupied by Native Americans. Other items found included a double-edged fine-toothed bone comb, a mirror and child-related artifacts such as the fragment of a porcelain doll's face and marbles.

The historical society undertook the tedious process of restoring the structure. A front porch that once stood on the dwelling's front façade was removed due to serious deterioration and repairs were made to various portions of the interior space and foundation.

Evidence of a massive fire that all but destroyed the 1769 structure was found in charcoal layers surrounding the house. The structure that exists today was rebuilt on the original foundation in 1814.

Now operating as a museum under the care of the historical society, many of the artifacts collected during the excavations are on display in the house to shed light on the history of the Dubois family, the house and the community.

The Andries Dubois Museum opened to the public in 2015. Displays in its front parlors include items from a local one-room schoolhouse and rotating exhibitions of local history.

The first room is named in honor of Hazel E. Ronk, a longtime Wallkill teacher who spent her first ten years of teaching in the one-room schoolhouse. The room contains desks, books and other memorabilia from vintage schoolhouses throughout the region.

The second room, honoring Mary Dubois Wright, a twelfth-generation Dubois family descendent, has been restored to a late 19th century and early 20th century appearance and provides a showcase for revolving exhibitions, including paintings and other original artifacts that represent the family.

The Andries Dubois Museum is open on Saturdays, April to October, from 10 a.m.-noon or by appointment. Call Harold van Aken at 845-895-3321 to schedule a visit.

The Andries Dubois House is located at 75 Wallkill Ave., Wallkill.

Beth David Synogogue

While not nearly as large or well known as the Jewish vacation resorts once found in the Catskill Mountains dubbed "the Borscht Belt," the Town of Amenia in Dutchess County once boasted its own thriving vacation community. It was established during the 1920s following the arrival of a number of Russian Jewish families who had relocated from Ellsworth, Connecticut, to Amenia to escape the anti-Semitism they'd encountered in nearby Sharon, Connecticut.

R.R. Colgate of the wealthy Colgate-Palmolive company lived at Filston, a beautiful estate in Sharon. Unfortunately, he was not fond of Jewish people and as a result of his influence they were not allowed to buy property there. Instead, they settled in Ellsworth, where they primarily engaged in farming.

Living in that community was difficult for them because they had to bus their children to different locales for better schooling. They soon discovered that they could relocate to nearby Amenia, New York, where there was a good school and railroad service.

Given the new opportunities afforded to them in New York, some became pharmacists and accountants, while others opened hotels and boardinghouses near Lake Amenia. With the availability of railroad service from New York City, many people would travel north to spend an entire summer in an efficiency cottage.

Caramoor

L ocated in Katonah, one of three hamlets in the Town of Bedford, Westchester County, sits Caramoor, the elegant summer estate of Walter and Lucie Rosen of New York City. Walter Tower Rosen made his fortune as an international banker and lawyer, while his wife came from a prominent New York family. They met in 1914 and, having instantly fallen in love, they married just six weeks later.

Walter Rosen was an astute art collector and musician, interests shared by his wife. Walter was a talented pianist who initially considered pursuing that career path. Lucie took up the violin while attending Royal Victoria College and the Royal Conservatory in Canada.

She made her formal debut in New York City in 1908 and attended a number of debutante balls that followed. She'd been on her own for some time but, during the summer of 1914, Lucie agreed to visit her mother and stepfather at their summer home in Canada. Her brother John invited a friend, Walter Rosen to join him for the weekend journey and despite their age difference – Walter was 39 and Lucie was 24 – it was love at first sight.

Within the first three years of their marriage, the couple had two children and settled into life at their Manhattan townhouse. Given their shared passion for music and the arts, the couple entertained some of the finest musicians, composers, authors, actors and directors at their house parties.

By 1928, they decided to buy a country estate north of the city to use on weekends and during summer months. By coincidence, Walter Rosen learned that his law partner, Charles Hoyt's mother Caroline, was in the process of selling her estate – named Caramoor, after her. Spanning one hundred acres in Katonah, it included an arts and crafts house and beautiful gardens. The couple immediately purchased it.

They did not care for the Hoyt residence itself, though, so between 1928 and 1939 the couple oversaw construction of a grand Mediterranean Revival villa on the property. The main house is a huge, pale yellow stucco building that features a red tiled roof. Primarily a two-story structure, its shape is almost square and includes a square ventral courtyard in its center. An outdoor terrace with a stone balustrade extends off the elegant dining room on its east side while a similar terrace extends from the master bedroom on the south side.

A distinctive arched gate along the south wall leads visitors through an iron gate and into the central courtyard, named the Spanish Courtyard, which is surrounded by various doorways that allow access to all the principal rooms on the first level of the house. Many of the interior rooms contain artwork, furnishings and other items collected by the Rosens during their frequent trips overseas. There are entire rooms that boast the styles and furnishings of countries such as Italy, France, Spain and England.

The home includes about twenty bathrooms that date to the Rosens' occupancy. Measuring forty feet by eighty feet with a thirty-foot high ceiling, the music room is the largest space in the house. Its coffered wood ceiling is 16th-century Italian, designed in the form of stars and crosses with rosettes in the center. The room boasts 16th-century French and Swiss stained glass and a pair of 16th-century marble columns that once belonged to William Randolph Hearst. The second floor is a much simpler design, featuring the bedrooms.

The grounds on the estate are stunning and include a sunken garden (installed by Caroline Hoyt), a tennis pavilion, hired help's living quarters, a stable, greenhouse and cottage, along with other outbuildings. Landscape features such as gazebos, a 19th- century cast iron garden urn and an assortment of trees and shrubs can be seen throughout the grounds.

In 1944, Walter got word that his namesake son, who was serving in the war overseas, had died of injuries sustained when his plane crashed. Shortly after receiving the tragic news the Rosens decided to bequeath Caramoor after their deaths as a center for music and the arts, in memory of their son. Two years later, the first concert was held in the music room.

Walter Rosen conceived the idea of building an outdoor theater, but he died in 1951 before the project was completed. Lucie continued to oversee its construction and, in 1958, it opened with a concert performance by contralto Marian Anderson. That night, the venue was christened the Venetian Theater.

In 1971, three years after Lucie Rosen died, Caramoor was opened to the public. Now known as Caramoor Center for Music and the Arts, the estate stages a wide range of concerts and other performances. The house is also open for tours so that art enthusiasts can see the world-class art that graces each room's walls. Special events, such as afternoon tea parties, are also held.

Caramoor is located at 149 Girdle Ridge Road, Katonah. For information about house tours, concerts and other functions, call 914-232-1252.

Chuang Yen Monastery

In 1964, the Buddhist Association of the United States (BAUS) was founded by Venerable Lok To, Chia-Tsin Shen and the latter's wife, Woo Ju Shen, all from China. It was a time of unrest in the country, with violent protests over the unpopular Vietnam War. The Buddhist Association's founders were motivated to develop the new source of spiritual illumination for the growing number of people who were searching for answers and a sense of peace.

As BAUS began to grow, its founders purchased an office building at 3070 Albany Crescent in the Bronx in 1969. The building had formerly served as a telephone company headquarters. After a complete renovation, it became the Temple of Enlightenment, which continues to teach Buddhist practices and provides service to Dharma students in New York City.

In 1975, the association acquired a 125-acre tract of land in Carmel, Putnam County, and six years later started construction on the monastic buildings that make up the Chuang Yen Monastery. The land was in fact leased to the association by Chia-Tsin Shen for a term of ninety-nine years at the cost of $1 per year. Shen eventually donated the property to the association in 1989.

In May 1981, a ground-breaking ceremony took place for the first building at the monastery – Kuan-Yin Hall. Through the years, other buildings were added including a dining hall, the Thousand Lotus Memorial Terrace, Tai-Hsu Hall, the Woo-Ju Memorial Library, Yin-Kuang Hall and the Great Buddha Hall. The Seven Jewel Lake and Lake and Bodhi Path were also created on the grounds.

The Great Buddha Hall, also known as the Hall of Ten Thousand Buddhas Encircling Buddha Vairocana, stands eighty-four feet tall, has an interior space of twenty-four thousand square feet and is capable of accommodating two thousand people in the main hall. World renowned architect I.M. Pei was a consultant on the project.

Undoubtedly, the primary attraction at the monastery is the thirty-seven foot statue of the Buddha Vairocana, which is the largest indoor Buddha statue in the western hemisphere. Surrounding the large Buddha statue are 10,000 small Buddha statues, which were fabricated by Professor C.G. Chen and stand on a lotus terrace.

A 104-foot long by 8-foot high mural covers the wall of the lotus terrace and depicts scenes from the "Pure Land" or "Western Paradise" of Amitabha Buddha. A larger mural, 144 feet long by 8 feet high, is displayed at the back of the terrace. It depicts 500 Arahants (people liberated from all defilements and impurities).

Completed in 1985, Kuan Yin Hall is used throughout the year to stage special ceremonies and functions such as seven-day meditation retreats, summer camp, and an activity center for English speaking programs. In the interior space, enclosed in a wooden shrine is a seven hundred-year-old porcelain statue of Kuan-Yin Bodhisattva that dates from the Ming dynasty.

In close proximity to the porcelain statue is a wooden one that depicts Kuan-Yin, which is one thousand years old. The six-foot tall statue underwent extensive restoration when it was received by the monastery.

Seven Jewels Lake was developed in a five-acre swampy area on the grounds, and it symbolizes the treasures of the Dharma. Adjacent to the lake is a ten-foot statue of Kuan-Yin. The area around the lake boasts walking paths, Chinese pavilions, decorative bridges and a beautiful rock garden.

The Chuang Yen Monastery is open to the public from April 1 through Jan. 2. It is located at 2020 Route 301, Carmel. The Bodhi

Path ("Path to Awakening") runs directly from the visitors' parking lot to the Great Buddha Hall. The path is graced by eighteen statues of Arahants, who were great disciples of the Buddha.

The dining hall also provides a vegetarian lunch for the general public on Saturdays and Sundays during the public visitation season. A $6 donation per person for lunch is requested.

David Crawford House

The 19th-century neo-classical mansion at 189 Montgomery St. in the City of Newburgh, Orange County was built in 1830 as the home of prominent shipping businessman David Crawford. The richly ornamented sixty-four-square-foot home, which features four forty-foot iconic columns at its entrance, reflects Crawford's stature and wealth.

On what was then a five hundred-acre estate overlooking the Hudson River, Crawford lived at the stately house with his wife, Fanny Belknap Crawford, and the couple's two daughters, Mary Elizabeth and Ann. Among the structure's distinctive characteristics includes front and rear Palladian windows, beautifully designed woodcarvings on the front door and throughout its interior, and ornate black marble fireplaces that heated the house with coal.

A newel post stylized image of a dolphin carved in solid mahogany graces the house's center hall staircase.

An artillery captain during the War of 1812, Crawford returned to Newburgh in 1817 to resume work in the mercantile and shipping business started by his father Francis. Young Crawford would play a significant role in transforming the small riverside community into a thriving shipping port and industrial city.

When Crawford began his career, the shipping industry used sloops to move cargo but, in 1830, he purchased the Baltimore, the first steamboat to operate from the Newburgh waterfront. Three years later, as his business grew, he added a second steamer named the Washington.

A progressive businessman at a time when freight barges replaced steamboats in river commerce, Crawford was quick to introduce two barges of his own – the Minisink and the Newburgh – into his fleet. He experienced considerable success with the enterprise and, at one point, he owned one-third of the entire waterfront in the city.

An influential civic leader, Crawford was a proponent of bringing the railroad to Newburgh. He was also instrumental in the establishment of the city's first cotton mill and the construction of North and South Plank roads. He also founded the Quassaick Bank and Newburgh Gas and Light Company.

A popular personality, Crawford enjoyed entertaining guests in his home and both of his daughters' weddings took place there. Positioned at the corner of Montgomery and Clinton streets, the home remains remarkably unchanged since Crawford's residency.

David Crawford died in 1856. By the time the 1929 stock market crash and subsequent Great Depression overwhelmed the nation, his house was owned by the Dietrich family. Three of the family's four children remained unmarried and living in the stately house until 1953, when they all mysteriously passed away with forty-five days of each other. Prior to their curious deaths, the siblings were forced to open the house to two boarders in order to make ends meet; one lived in the dining room and study while the other occupied space that is today a gift shop.

Following the Dietrich siblings' deaths, a local funeral home attempted to purchase the grand old house with plans to demolish it and create a parking lot for its business. Distressed over its proposed fate, the local historical society quickly raised the necessary funds to buy the house for use as its new headquarters.

Part of Newburgh's historic district, the largest in New York State, Crawford House remains the only 19th-century residence in the city that is open to the public on a regular basis. Today, under the auspices of the Historical Society of Newburgh Bay and the Highlands, the majestic house is interpreted to reflect both the home of a wealthy 19th- century family and also the rich history and traditions of Newburgh's past.

Visitors will find a display of Hudson River School paintings, 18th-century furniture and a collection of model ships that represent the heyday of pleasure travel and the thriving shipping industry that existed along the Hudson River.

For more information about public tours, which are conducted April through October, along with upcoming events and functions held at the house, contact the society at 845-562-1195.

Derick Brinckerhoff Mansion

Perched atop a bluff at the juncture of Route 82 and Route 52, two miles east of the Village of Fishkill sits the Brinckerhoff mansion, a structure that had its beginnings in 1718. That year, Dirck Brinckerhoff purchased a two hundred-acre tract of land from Madam Brett. Shortly thereafter, his son Abraham constructed two stone rooms, which eventually became the southwest ground floor of the home.

Madam Catharyna Brett inherited 28,000 acres in Dutchess County, a third-share of the Rombout Patent acquired by her father, Francis Rombout, and two partners in 1683 from the Wappinger Indians. Following the death of her husband, Roger Brett, in 1718, she began to sell off portions of the vast land holding to sustain her family.

Just prior to the Revolutionary War, Abraham's son Derick enlarged the home considerably by erecting a mansion around the original two room structure.

The family operated a grist mill along the nearby Fishkill Creek, and a store just west of the home. Upon Abraham Brinkerhoff's death in 1738, the home and businesses were inherited by Derick, who prospered financially. He also became immersed in county affairs.

He served as a member of the Provincial Assembly from 1768 to 1777 was a delegate to the first Provincial Congress, was chairman of the Committee for Safety in the Rombout Precinct and served as a colonel of the militia.

In August 1776, the Brinckerhoff store became the focus of one hundred angry women from Fishkill and Beekman. Led by Catharine Schutt, they stormed the business and demanded that they be sold tea at the "lawful price" of six shillings. Brinckerhoff feared the destruction of the tea in stock and wisely defused the situation by meeting the women's demands. Their actions were similar to the political protest orchestrated by the Sons of Liberty in Boston three years earlier.

The location of the Brinckerhoff house made it an ideal stopping place during the war. In January 1777, while traveling to Philadelphia, John Adams stayed there for one night. In March 1778 the home served as headquarters for Continental Army General Alexander McDougall, who was conducting an investigation there to determine the cause of the army's devastating losses at Fort Clinton and Fort Montgomery five months earlier.

Among visitors to the home during the inquiry were New York Governor George Clinton, John Jay, General Henry Knox and Benedict Arnold.

General George Washington stayed at the Brinckerhoff house from Oct. 1-8, 1778, and was accompanied by a staff that included Alexander Hamilton. He ate breakfast at the house on the morning that he received word about General Benedict Arnold's collusion with British Major John Andre for the British takeover of West Point, which Arnold commanded at the time. The plan failed when Andre was captured in Tarrytown, Westchester County, on his way back to British lines.

French General Marques de Lafayette stayed at the home during part of Washington's visit and stopped by again three weeks later after a trip to Philadelphia. But on his return visit, the French general fell seriously ill and was confined in a second floor bedroom in the Brinckerhoff home for an entire month.

When Lafayette became ill, Washington sent for his personal physician, Dr. Cochran, to treat the French general. The kindness of the Brinckerhoff family caring for him was not lost on Lafayette and, in 1824, when he visited the United States again he presented the family with an elegant French-made period desk in gratitude for their earlier hospitality.

Following the American Revolution, Derick Brinckerhoff stayed active in local politics and soon became the sheriff of Dutchess County.

For nearly three centuries, Brinckerhoff descendants have maintained ownership and residency in the house. It was updated during the 19th century by Matthew Brinckerhoff, who covered the stone exterior with wood siding, replaced the original fireplace mantles with marble ones and added a mansard roof to make room for five bedrooms on the third floor.

In 2014, Mary Brinckerhoff sold the ten thousand-square-foot mansion. Following renovations, it is now operating as the Brinckerhoff Inn, a bed and breakfast. Mindful of its historic value, the new owner retained its original wood floors, plaster walls, doors, Crown molding and stairs. Many pieces of art, photographs and historical documents that once belonged to the Brinckerhoff family adorn the walls of the structure.

Adjacent to the west side of the Brinckerhoff property is the old Presbyterian Church graveyard, now Rombout Rural Cemetery. While the church no longer exists on the site, it was used during the American Revolution as a military hospital. There are a number of unmarked graves of Continental Army soldiers who perished in the war on the site.

On May 30, 1898, the Melzingah Chapter of the Daughters of the American Revolution erected a monument in the cemetery to honor Lafayette; it sits along Route 52.

For more information, contact the inn at 845-765-2535 or visit online at www.brinckerhoffinn.com.

Desmond Estate

Located on a hillside on the east side of Albany Post Road in Balmville, a hamlet in the Town of Newburgh, is an estate that was first established in the early 19th century by Samuel Betts, a distinguished judge in New York. His dwelling consisted of a small house that he had built on the property.

Following the War of 1812, Captain Robinson, who was an officer on the frigate USS Constitution, purchased the Betts estate and enhanced the house by installing marble mantelpieces, which he acquired in Italy and had shipped home. After Robinson died, the estate was purchased in 1882 by Edward A. Wickes.

Wickes immediately tore down the original house and had a wood-frame mansion with a distinctive cupola built in its place. Before demolishing the previous house, he salvaged the mantelpieces that Robinson had installed and incorporated them into the new structure, which he named Krans Kop, a Dutch saying that means "rounded hilltop."

Wickes chose the name because of its scenic location high above the Hudson River. A number of estates were established during the 18th and 19th centuries in Balmville including Algonac, home of the Warren Delano family. Sara Delano would become the future mother of President Franklin D. Roosevelt. Algonac was located just east of Krans Kop, closer to the river.

After spending just eight years at Krans Kop, Wickes and his family relocated again in 1891, this time to an adjacent estate named Morningside, which was in his family's ownership for many years and featured a home constructed of Gothic brick. Kraus Kop remained either vacant or rented for some time and eventually had one other owner, William Beal, before it was again put up for sale.

In 1930, Thomas and Alice (Curtis) Desmond, two accomplished and wealthy residents from New York City, purchased the estate. The mansion had served its previous owners as a vacation home, but the Desmonds, planned to live there full time, and so had the mansion winterized. Thomas Desmond was an engineer and New York State Senator while his wife Alice was an author, artist and photographer.

The couple enjoyed a full life at Krans Kop and, due to their very productive and varied careers, they traveled extensively through the years. The mansion included an extensive library, the senator's office and Alice Desmond's beloved third-floor art studio, where she engaged in her first love, painting.

While Alice's passion was painting, her father only permitted her to study commercial art, which in his view had practical applications. Upon marrying Thomas Desmond, she discovered that her husband had little appreciation for art and always wanted to marry a writer. To please him, Alice studied writing and eventually became an award-winning author. While living on the Balmville estate, Alice Desmond authored more than twenty books, primarily historical biographies.

Senator Desmond's interest in botany motivated him to cultivate 850 varieties of trees and shrubs on the estate, which, in time, led the estate to becoming well-known as a beautiful arboretum.

The couple, who never had children, decorated their new home in a manner that preserved its historical character. Because Judge Betts maintained a color scheme of white clapboard and green trim, the Desmonds had the mansion painted in that manner. An adjacent parcel of land included a vintage cemetery where some of the area's earliest settlers were interred; the Desmonds purchased the land and erected an iron gate around the burial site.

Senator Desmond passed away in October 1972, at the age of eighty-five. Four years later, Alice Desmond, at seventy-nine years of age, married for a second time, this time to former U.S. Congressman Hamilton Fish lll of the prestigious New York family. Despite the couple's hope to enjoy growing old together, the marriage quickly fell apart and ended in divorce in 1984.

Alice Desmond died in October 1990, at the age of ninety-three. Because the Desmonds never had children, she bequeathed her estate to Mount Saint Mary College, whose main campus is located just a few miles south in the City of Newburgh.

The Desmond Campus, as the estate is now known, houses the Center for Community and Educational Services and accommodates special events. The programs offered there support the goals of the college in providing learning opportunities and enrichment for adult residents of the greater Hudson Valley. Non-credit classes on a wide variety of topics are offered days, evenings and on Saturdays year-round. Several bus trips every year focus on the arts and history.

The Desmond Campus is located at 6 Albany Post Road, Balmville. For more information about classes and trips, call 845-565-2076.

District #9 School House

Courtesy of Kathleen L. Alevras

While there are no existing documents to verify the date that the District #9 Schoolhouse in the Town of Goshen was built, its current owner – the Minisink Chapter of the Daughters of the American Revolution (DAR) – believe that it was sometime between 1730 and 1740. An 1843 fire in the municipal building that contained early documents from the town all but destroyed all the records stored inside.

In 1723, prominent country resident Charles Howell, who owned an adjacent farm, donated a portion of his property for the construction of a one-room schoolhouse to serve the rural communities of Howell and Finnegan's Corners. The one-story, stone building was commonly referred to as the Borden School due to its close proximity to the creamery owned by the Borden family.

It was also known as the Quarry School because of a limestone quarry that was located two miles away. Originally called the Dutchess Quarry, it is now owned by Tilcon. In the school's heyday, teachers took the students on field trips to visit the nearby caves, which are known for having artifacts (stone points) that were left by the Paleo Indians more than twelve thousand years ago.

Surrounded by a rural landscape despite its close proximity to

Hezekiah developed a successful farm operation on the site.

Following DuBois's death in 1767, the house and farm were left to his son David, who in turn sold it to Christopher Kiersted in 1773. Kiersted became the first doctor to settle in the Village of Saugerties. When the physician died in 1791, the property was passed along to his son, John. It was John who planted the black locust trees in front of the house. He also added the Georgian detailing that now enhances the house's appearance.

John Kiersted studied surveying and eventually chose it as his career. He was held in high esteem for his work and engaged in multiple projects for the Hardenburgh family, whose land holdings spanned Ulster, Delaware, Greene and Sullivan counties. Kiersted also worked with other prominent land holders in the region including the Livingston family. Kiersted also became involved with tanning and lead manufacturing and in politics. He was elected to the New York State Assembly in 1814.

The interior of the house boasts a center hall that is flanked by two large parlors. The entire first level features wide-plank floors. The walls on that level feature plaster on stone finishes and other amenities include Georgian moldings, doors and iron hardware throughout. It is likely that during Kiersted's occupancy during the early 19th century, the house was expanded again.

The second floor of the dwelling is divided into several small rooms, which were modernized throughout its history. The house features a steeply pitched roof, and a number of dormers have been added to it in more recent times. The back porch and present kitchen are thought to be the last additions to the house.

The dwelling was slated for demolition in 1955. However, through the efforts of local residents Charles and Inez Steele and with the support of volunteers who worked closely with town and village officials, the Saugerties Historical Society purchased the historic stone house in 1998. In 2001, the society secured a $150,000 grant to renovate the house, which now serves as a museum.

The Dubois-Kiersted Stone House is open to the public May through October on Saturdays from 11 a.m.-2 p.m. and Sundays from 1-4 p.m. It is located at 119 Main St., Saugerties.

Estherwood

James Jennings McComb was born in Mansfield, Ohio, in 1829. He worked as a real estate investor in New Orleans, London, England and New York, all cities where he resided at one time. But it wasn't until he invented the tie that secured bales of cotton as they emerged from cotton bailing machines that he gained great wealth.

McComb set down roots in Dobbs Ferry, New York, in 1860, when he purchased a twenty-three-acre parcel of land from Dr. Ryder. At the time, the community boasted several grand estates.

From its inception, McComb provided financial support for the Misses Masters School, as it was originally known. Founded as an all-girls school by Eliza Bailey Masters in 1877, three of McComb's daughters attended the school. He moved his family into a house known as Park Cottage on Clinton Avenue to be close to the school.

McComb added an octagonal library to the residence specifically to house an octagonal desk that he had purchased in Europe. But the addition did not fit well with the modest appearance of the residence.

In 1894, McComb commissioned the New York City architectural firm of Buchman and Deisler to design a mansion for him to be built around the new library. He had the rest of the original home moved to a tract of land down the street.

The result of Buchman and Deisler's effort was a stunning 3½-story French Chateauesque mansion built of white pressed brick with Jonesville granite trim and a porte cochere and veranda that feature Guastavino ceilings. Guastavino tile is a tile arch system that was patented in the United States in 1885 by Spanish architect and builder Rafael Guastavino. It is known for its structural and aesthetic appearance.

The mansion is the only structure of its kind in all of Westchester County. McComb christened it Estherwood.

The building has fifteen dormers, an oriel window protruding from the structure on its second floor and four brick chimneys on a distinctive black and red ceramic tile roof. The main floor consists of six large formal rooms, including a sixty-five-foot Great Hall that is a two-story space topped by two skylights. A dining room fitted with dark oak paneling and a music room, the latter also known as the Red Room, features an alcove on its northern wall that is flanked by red marble columns.

A reception room – called the Gold Room – features two windows that have gold stained glass panels and a brass and crystal chandelier. The library has an octagonal skylight centered in its ceiling. A billiard room rounds out the first level. Several bedrooms are in the upper floors.

A powerful generator was installed in the mansion's basement. It had the capacity to supply power for one thousand electric lights, a swimming pool, a bowling alley and a cistern from which rain water could be recycled to a nearby greenhouse. A Queen Anne-style carriage house was built just east of the mansion and still exists there today.

When it was completed in 1895, the residence was so opulent that it was compared to The Breakers, one of the many Vanderbilt family's homes in Newport, Rhode Island. That home was designed by renowned architect Richard Morris Hunt and was completed just three years before Estherwood was built.

McComb acquired the surrounding parcels of land through his years of residency at Estherwood and rented some of the land to Misses Masters School, later to be incorporated as The Masters School. He

scouting and skirmishes between the Rapidan and Rappahannock as part of General William Averell's cavalry division. His letters home to his mother described a number of visits that he had spent with his brother while serving. Sadly, he received word of Edward's death while on guard duty and it was his fate to share the news with his mother.

By July 1863, John Ketchem was determined to be too exhausted for duty and he was sent to the Seminary Hospital in Georgetown, Washington DC. He spent four weeks there under the care of his mother, Martha Ketcham, who traveled alone from Milton to care for her only living son. John eventually got orders to report for duty as part of Devin's Brigade under General John Buford's cavalry division the last week of August. With that unit, John Ketchem was engaged in daily skirmishes with southern troops and, while stationed in Raccoon Ford, Virginia, he and another twenty-three troops were captured by the Confederate Army.

Confined at Libby Prison in Richmond, Virginia, with a number of his fellow officers, John Ketchem succumbed to a combination of his failing health along with the filth and disease prevalent in the prison. He was transferred to the prison hospital, where he died Oct. 8, 1863. Sometime after the war ended, Martha Ketchem traveled south to claim the bodies of her two sons.

Both Edward and John Ketchem were reinterred side by side in one of Milton's two Quaker burial grounds. The siblings' two white monuments still stand at the Friends' Hicksites Quaker Cemetery, located on a hillside at the southwest corner of Route 9W and Willow Tree Road, Milton, behind an active commercial business.

*The Ketchems' cousin, Nehemiah Hallock Mann's gravestone
features a stone captain's hat.*

Just to the east of the Ketchem brothers' monuments sits the grave
of their cousin, Captain Mann, whose gravestone marker is topped
with a stone captain's hat.

First Columbia County Courthouse

Located on the north side of Route 23B at its intersection with Old Lane in Claverack, one of several hamlets in the Town of Claverack, Columbia County is a two-story, five-bay by four-bay brick building that served as the county's first courthouse, from 1786 through 1805. Claverack was the county seat at that time.

The parcel of land designated for the courthouse's construction was deeded to the county's board of supervisors by Gabriel Esselstyne on June 7, 1786 at the cost of £20. Work commenced on the project a month later, and the four workers tasked with digging the building's cellar were provided with housing by Esselstyne, for which he was compensated.

Within days of the project's start, stones began to arrive at the site; a number of local residents helped move the heavy building material. The project took two years to complete and was constructed under the watchful eye of local businessman William H. Ludlow; the bricks used in the building came from Ludlow's nearby kiln.

In addition to the three courtrooms that occupied the upper level, the building also included the offices of the county clerk and surrogate. The final cost of the building came to £9,000. At the time, the judicial system was based on the colonial courts and both the first court of common appeals and court of general sessions opened in Claverack on Jan. 9, 1797.

The courthouse included a small jail in the rear of the building. A pillory that was used for public whippings, as well as a hanging tree for those sentenced to death were on the courthouse grounds; neither remains on the site today.

The first judge to oversee a trial in the building was attorney Peter Van Ness of Kinderhook. Among the prominent attorneys who tried cases in the new building were Alexander Hamilton, Aaron Burr and future U.S. President Martin Van Buren. Van Buren, another native of Kinderhook, completed his legal studies and training in Van Ness's office in 1802.

In 1839 while in office, President Van Buren purchased Van Ness's former mansion in Kinderhook, naming it Lindenwald. It is now open for public tours and is featured in volume 2 of the Hidden Treasures of the Hudson Valley series.

Hamilton gained fame for his representation in the appeal trial of Harry Croswell, in what became one of the country's most famous libel trials. In 1802, Croswell was sued for libel by then sitting U.S. President Thomas Jefferson. The trial became an important case in the evolution of the nation's defamation law.

The genesis of the lawsuit was based on Croswell's support of John Adams' Federalist Party over that of Jefferson's Democratic-Republicans. As a journalist, Croswell wrote numerous pro-Adams articles touting that stance in the Balance and Columbian Repository, a local newspaper. Croswell eventually convinced his editor to allow him to establish a new publication, The Wasp, in order to attack the writings of another county reporter, Charles Holt, who was just as eager to support the Republicans in his newspaper, The Bee. Croswell however, wrote articles in The Wasp under the pseudonym Robert Risticoat. The two journalists engaged in vicious exchanges over several months.

When, in a September 1802 issue of The Wasp, Croswell attacked Jefferson, stating that the president paid Virginian James Thomson Callender to print negative remarks about Adams in The Richmond Recorder (and also called the late U.S. President George Washington "a traitor, robber and perjurer") the remarks captured the attention of New York Attorney General Ambrose Spencer.

Two days after the article was printed, Croswell was arrested and taken to the Columbia County Courthouse in Claverack. His libel trial began on July 11, 1803, with Supreme Court Justice Morgan Lewis – a well-known anti-Federalist – presiding. Although Croswell was represented pro bono by a team of prominent attorneys, including Van Ness, he was found guilty.

Hamilton, who was unavailable to participate in the original trial, made a six-hour statement at his appeal. The ultimate verdict ended in a tie but Croswell was never sentenced and though a new trial was ordered, it never occurred. It ended with the case never being disposed.

The Claverack Courthouse continued to serve the county until 1805, when the court system relocated to Hudson. The vacant Claverack building was subsequently used as a school and a dance hall. In 1843, Peter Hoffman, a retired merchant from Brooklyn, purchased the building and converted it into a private residence. After Hoffman's occupancy, four other private owners – all from New York City – acquired the building, which went through a series of restorations and modifications.

During the late 1940s, a new owner transformed the house into a multi-unit apartment dwelling, which it remains today. The historic building is located at 549 Route 23B, Claverack (now Hudson).

Firthcliffe Firehouse

Near the end of the 19th century, water power originating from the Moodna Creek near Canterbury (today the Town of Cornwall) was channeled for use by the Firthcliffe Mills, a large carpet manufacturer. Owned and operated by a Charles Firthcliffe, who was described during the early 1900s as a paternalistic employer, he also built a series of modest dwellings for his employees, as well as a stately home for himself near the mill.

Firthcliffe immigrated to the United States from Scotland and established his mill in 1886. It manufactured and sold quality carpets all over the world. The Cornwall operation had 500 employees at the height of its production's output.

The neighborhood around the mill, including employee housing came to be known as the unincorporated Village of Firthcliffe. In 1910, a three-bay square brick firehouse was built along Willow Avenue for the protection of the mill, employee houses and Mr. Firthcliffe's residence.

Other businesses, such as a post office, general store and a train station, quickly sprang up in the small community. In 1903, the carpet company built a clubhouse for its employees, which featured a pool, card room, billiard table and reading room on the first floor and a gym and dance floor on the second level. Its basement was equipped with bowling alleys. The clubhouse was destroyed by a massive fire in 1970.

Through the years, a number of the private employee residences built by Firthcliffe have survived but appear very different today due to various exterior changes and additions made by subsequent owners.

On the other hand, the Firthcliffe Firehouse remains the last standing remnant of that earlier period in village history, the mill itself also long gone. Made of American bond brick, the firehouse was built to house one fire engine, which suggests that it was only intended to protect the immediate vicinity rather than a large geographic area.

Situated on a small parcel of land on the north side of Willow Avenue, the firehouse had one wide engine door in its center, a square bell tower and a bell-shaped gable that extends out over the engine door entrance. It was built during a period when Cornwall was experiencing its first burst of commercial development. Boasting a hip slate roof, stone lintels and sills and tall casement windows, the integrity of the structure remains intact today. The overall design of the building suggests a Queen Anne style.

The interior of the firehouse was one big room. Its fire pole, which enabled firefighters resting upstairs to quickly slide down to the main level and the fire engine, is still in place. The entrance to the basement is located on the exposed south side of the firehouse because the property slopes downward from the road to the rear of the building. A simple wooden staircase leads to the basement as well as to the bell tower.

The firehouse eventually closed and the building has been occupied by various business ventures through the years. Today it's home to a hair salon. The building's wide central engine door has been replaced by a bay window.

The picturesque Firthcliffe Firehouse is located at 196 Willow Ave., Cornwall.

Fish And Fur Club

The Fish and Fur Club was organized in 1895 in the Village of Nelsonville, Town of Philipstown, Putnam County, by a group of local hunters, trappers and fishermen. Initially, the men met at the house of L. W. Jaycox, one of the original fourteen founding members of the club.

John Henyen was elected the club's first president and bylaws were agreed on and documented. In the beginning, the club had no funds to work with and soon fell into debt just purchasing a few tables and chairs to use during meetings.

It cost 25 cents to join the club and 10 cents per week dues were charged to build its initial financial standing. If a member failed to pay dues for fifteen consecutive weeks, his membership was terminated.

However, the club grew in membership. After meeting at the Jaycox house for three years, the group moved to the George Seedling building at the corner of Main and Division streets. The club met at that location from 1898 until 1905 when the members purchased a vacant lot at the corner of Main and Pearl streets from Josiah Ferris, a club member.

Immediately following the purchase, the club members started to sell bonds to raise funds for the construction of a new clubhouse. When the money was raised, they hired Martin Adams, a local contractor, to build the one-story, three-bay by three-bay frame building on a stone foundation, at a final cost of $1,500. Completed in fall 1905, a raccoon supper was held for members, their families and friends to celebrate the official opening of the new clubhouse.

Sometime after taking occupancy in the building, the Fish and Fur Club was incorporated. When Phoenix Shaffer was elected its new president, he vowed to focus on paying off the outstanding bonds. The majority of the outstanding bonds were held by Steward Jaycox, the club's treasurer, and he donated the interest due him back to the club and closed the bonds for the value he originally paid for them. However, it wasn't until June 1943 that Jaycox received his settlement check and the matter of outstanding bonds was finally closed.

Under yet another president, Edward Collard, weekly game parties were held in the clubhouse and were enthusiastically supported by the community. Through this initiative and due to the tireless work by club members at the functions, the parties raised significant funds, enough to take the club out of debt.

The clubhouse was used by the Nelsonville Fire Department in 1923 to hold its first meeting. That group continued to meet there until the construction of a firehouse down the street was completed in 1955.

The Fish and Fur Club remained active at the clubhouse through the late 1950s when a deal was brokered with the village to swap buildings; the club relocated to a building next door while the municipality acquired the clubhouse to serve as its justice court, the office of the village clerk and a meeting room for the village board.

Village Hall (the Former Fish and Fur Club) is located at 258 Main St., Nelsonville.

General Hathorn Stone House

Located on the north side of today's Hathorn Road in the Town of Warwick, Orange County sits a 1½-story stone house that once belonged to a military officer during the American Revolution. It was once part of a three hundred-acre farm that was owned by General John Hathorn, who had designed and built the house in 1773. It is constructed of locally quarried stone and its interior floors consist of hewn planks of oak timber, some of them thirty inches wide.

On the west gable of the dwelling, the initials "J," "E," and "H," along with the year "1773" are set in brick into the stone exterior. They stand for John and Elizabeth Hathorn and the year the house was completed. The bricks used for the unusual monogram are said to have been imported from Holland.

Born in 1749 and trained as a surveyor and teacher, Hathorn arrived in Orange County when he was part of a crew involved with a project to identify the exact boundaries of New York and New Jersey. He settled in what is now Warwick in 1770 and was married within two years to Elizabeth Welling.

Originally commissioned a captain when the American Revolution began, Hathorn rose through the ranks. He was promoted to colonel in 1776 in charge of the Fourth Orange County Regiment and to Brigadier General ten years later with the same outfit. In 1793, he became a major general of the state militia and was said to have had an extremely close relationship with Continental Army General George Clinton, who became New York's first governor.

Hathorn's troops helped guard the Ramapo Mountains and Sterling Forest. They responded to alarms about Native American raiding parties along the Delaware frontier, and they fought at the Battle of White Plains. He had the distinction of helping to determine the placement of the great chain across the Hudson River at West Point, and it was his men who erected the buildings and fortifications in that area.

Having served on the Committee of Safety and Observation, stationed in the Hudson Valley, Hathorn was a member at the first session of the New York State Assembly in Kingston and Poughkeepsie. On July 22, 1779, Hathorn led his militia at the Battle of Minisink, the only major conflict to take place in that part of the region during the Revolutionary War.

The battle began when, two days earlier, a group of about ninety Loyalists and Iroquois Native Americans (allies of the British forces) descended upon the settlement of Peenpack (today's City of Port Jervis) and waged a vicious attack that left the community in ruins.

The attack was led by Mohawk war chief Joseph Brant, who also served as a captain in the British Army. When word of the attack reached Goshen, Orange County, outraged settlers in that community immediately formed a militia with the intention of pursuing Brant and his men in retribution for the brutal act.

Lieutenant Colonel Benjamin Tusten, commander of the militia was reluctant to move forward with the plan because of the Loyalists' capability and manpower, along with a shortage of trained men in Goshen to oppose them in battle.

Tusten eventually gave in to their demands for justice and led his men northward the following morning. They eventually joined forces with a portion of the Fourth Orange County Regiment that was ordered into action by George Washington and was led by Colonel John Hathorn. The combined number of Patriot troops totaled 120.

The militia set up on the hills above the Delaware River ready to wage an ambush, but when one militia officer fired a shot at one of Brant's men, alerting the opposition of their presence, Brant immediately began to outflank the Patriots. With his troops scattered and separated from Tusten's troops, Hathorn had no choice but to retreat. The battle was a decisive victory for the Loyalists.

Hathorn went on to serve as a member of the New York State Assembly periodically from 1778 to 1805. He was the speaker of the assembly in 1783 and 1784. He was also elected a two-term New York State senator as well as a state representative to the Continental Congress in 1778. He went on to win election to the first United States Congress in 1789 and served two terms in that role.

In 1822, upon finally receiving the remains of militiamen lost at the Battle of Minisink, seventy-three-year-old General John Hathorn was chosen to speak at a formal ceremony held in Goshen. He stated: "Monuments to the brave are mementos to their descendants. The honors they record are stars to the Patriot in the path of glory. Beneath the mausoleum whose foundation we now lay repose all that was earthly of patriots and heroes."

Hathorn died at his home in Warwick on Feb. 19, 1825, and his beloved residence was held in the family for another nine years, after which it was purchased by Ezra Sanford. The house remained in the Sanford family's care for the next ninety-seven years. Since 1924, the historic house has had three owners.

The John Hathorn House is now in the process of being converted into a fine dining facility. It is located at 21 Hathorn Road, Warwick.

German Reformed Church Parsonage

During the early 18th century, the War of the Spanish Succession led to countless numbers of German refugees relocating to England. Despite having origins in diverse areas, the British labeled them Palatines. By 1709, the massive influx of refugees presented challenges for England and its ability to handle them, which resulted in a plan to relocate many of them to the Hudson Valley in the Colony of New York.

In exchange for free passage across the Atlantic Ocean on ten British ships, the three thousand Palatines were expected to engage in harvesting pine trees near the Hudson River in order to make tar and pitch for the Royal Navy. Colonial Governor Robert Hunter purchased a six thousand-acre parcel of land in today's Germantown from Robert Livingston, whose family had huge land holdings in the region and who resided at the nearby Clermont estate.

After arriving in New York and going through a period of quarantine on today's Governor's Island just off the Manhattan shoreline, the Palatines were transported north on the Hudson River bound for the Mid-Hudson region.

Divided between two sites on the east and west sides of the river, the Palatine settlements were named East Camp and West Camp. The East Camp colony had four villages: Hunterstown, Queensbury,

Annsbury and Haysbury; the combined villages were later renamed Germantown, a name it retains today.

Despite the British plans, the operation failed within two years because officials soon learned that the climate and types of pine trees that would grow in New York were not conducive to meeting their needs. Therefore, the German Palatines transported from England were of no use to the Crown.

The camps quickly lost the financial support of the British Parliament and the German Palatines were left to fend for themselves in the New World. In 1712, the Palatines began to disperse throughout the region, settling in various communities up and down the river. Many became tenant farmers on property belonging to wealthy land owners.

While many relocated to other areas in New York, sixty-three families remained in East Camp. There, they erected the German (Calvinist) Reformed Sanctity Church during the 1720s. A church parsonage was built about two blocks east of the church in 1746, when the congregation hired its first resident pastor, Casper Ludwig Schnoor.

Johannes Casparus Rubel replaced Schnoor as pastor in 1751 and remained in residence at the parsonage through 1767, when the east section of the structure was added. While the original west section of the parsonage boasts three-foot wide exterior walls made of limestone, the east section is a brick-filled wood frame building. The building's front façade faces south on the north side of today's Maple Avenue, east of Route 9G.

Subsequent pastors resided at the parsonage well into the 19th century. A new Reformed Church was built in 1814 and the original structure succumbed to years of deterioration and was eventually torn down. The Palatines simply thought it was time to move farther inland because their population was growing.

In 1829, the parsonage building was purchased by Dr. Wessel Ten Broeck Van Orden, who lived there for the next twenty years. In 1852, African-American Henry Person purchased the building. Local lore passed down through generations has it that Person and his neighbors – the Robinson family – were former slaves who had worked in the area.

When the Person family sold the building to Henry Fingar in 1911, tenant families occupied the parsonage through Fingar's death in 1942. Two years later, Long Island residents Friedl and Edward Ekert purchased the parsonage and undertook a series of extensive renovations on the building.

They poured a concrete floor in the basement, put stucco on the front exterior of the building and installed a window where a door had previously been on the south façade. In 1990, the Ekerts donated the former parsonage to the Town of Germantown. It now houses the town historian's office and welcomes visitors on Saturdays year-round from 9 a.m.-noon.

The interior of the parsonage still boasts its original beams, built-in cabinets and doors, and a huge fireplace in what had been the first floor but is now considered the basement. The building houses an extensive exhibit of items found during a years-long dig led by archeologist Dr. Christopher Lindner of Bard College.

The former German Reformed Church Parsonage is located at 51 Maple Ave., Germantown.

Gilead Cemetery

The Gilead Cemetery in the Town of Carmel, Putnam County, was established in the mid-18th century with gravestones dating back to 1766. It is known for its vintage funerary art visible on sandstone, fieldstone and slate gravestones and for the number of prominent citizens interred there. Many of them had fought and died during the Revolutionary War.

Located off Mechanic Street, the cemetery is surrounded by a stone wall (likely erected simply to keep the livestock from surrounding farms out of the grounds) and two fieldstone gateposts that mark its entrance with two iron gates. It occupies approximately 1¼ acres that was originally leased by Thomas Crosby in 1756 from Frederick Philipse of Philipsburg Manor in Tarrytown, Westchester County. Because of Philipse's loyalty to the Crown during the American Revolution, he forfeited his massive land holdings, which were put up for sale, initially to tenant farmers who had previously paid rent to use the land.

A meeting house was established quickly and fifty-seven of the original congregation offered the position of pastor to Rev. Ebenezer Knibloe. He accepted and held the role for three years. He was followed by Elnathan Gregory, who stayed at Gilead Church for the next thirteen years. One of Gregory's well known and widely printed sermons titled "Is there no balm in Gilead" became the stimulus for the meeting house and cemetery's name.

The congregation used the fifty-foot by fifty-foot church at the west end of Gilead Cemetery from 1756 to 1839. Prior to 1774, the church was Congregational and communicated with the Old Congregational Church in Southeast and with another one near the Tilly Foster section of Carmel. In 1774, the Rev. David Close became Gilead's first Presbyterian pastor, simultaneously overseeing the Presbyterian Church in Patterson. Following his death in 1783 at just forty years of age, he was buried in the Patterson church's graveyard.

The first person interred at the Gilead Cemetery in 1766 was Sarah Smith. Her farm was leased to a new tenant farmer. Smith's stone was made of slate and features an inverted half-moon. Other gravestones during that time period typically were carved from sandstone and feature a variety of designs such as skulls, starbursts, skeletons and dead heads, all meant to represent the triumphant finality of death. By the late 19th century, carved cherub heads started to appear atop gravestones.

A number of American troops who perished in the Revolutionary War are buried in the cemetery, but undoubtedly the most famous person interred there is Enoch Crosby, the son of Thomas, who originally leased the land the cemetery occupies. Enoch Crosby was a double spy working for the Continental Army, and he was very skilled at entering British lines to learn their plans and report back to the Patriots.

Patriot spy Enoch Crosby's grave boasts the largest monument in the cemetery.

Only a select few officers knew of his status and on one occasion he was captured by Continental Army troops, who believed that he was a British spy. To protect his identity and mission, Crosby was detained and eventually tried in a mock trial held at the Van Wyck Homestead in Fishkill, after which he was quietly allowed to escape and return to his important work.

The incident generated the attention of famous American author James Fenimore Cooper, who wrote the book The Spy: A Tale of the Neutral Ground, fictionalizing Crosby's name as Harvey Birch in the book.

Despite being eventually uncovered, beaten and left for dead and, on another occasion, shot by a British soldier, Crosby survived and returned to Carmel after the war. He lived until 1835. His monument in Gilead Cemetery – one of the largest on the grounds – is topped by carved sword and musket, a tribute to his superior military service.

Local benefactor Ferdinand Hopkins was responsible for having the two pillars and gates installed at the cemetery's entrance and erecting Crosby's monument. Around the same time, the Gilead Cemetery Association was created to maintain its grounds and document its history.

When the larger and nearby Raymond Hill Cemetery opened in the early 19th century, burials at Gilead decreased significantly. Burials that took place at the Gilead Cemetery after the Raymond Hill Cemetery opened were likely descendants of previously interred family members. The last burial to take place at Gilead Cemetery was in 1959. The town now owns the cemetery ground.

The Gilead Cemetery is located at 29 Mechanic St. at Northgate Road.

Glebe House

Glebe House – the 1½-story, 18th-century Georgian-style red brick building at 635 Main St. in the City of Poughkeepsie, Dutchess County – was built in 1767 as a residence for the minister of both the Poughkeepsie and Fishkill Churches of England. It later served as a retail establishment.

Glebe is a Saxon word meaning "an area of land of which the proceeds supported the parish and provided a home to its minister to supplement his income."

In 1766, the Poughkeepsie church – now Christ Episcopal Church – joined a Fishkill congregation – Trinity Church – to share the services of one minister. When they approached the Society for the Propagation of the Gospel for approval, the combined congregations agreed to provide the minister with a house and property.

The Reverend John Beardsley was hired and it was his choice to reside either in Poughkeepsie or in Fishkill. When he chose to live in Poughkeepsie, the site on Main Street – then known as Filkintown Road – was purchased.

The combined parishes purchased the sixty-four-acre Ostrander farm in 1767 and the oldest (western) part of the house was built at that time. Another twenty-three acres were soon purchased. Then, in 1773, an additional two hundred acres was added by royal grant of "common lands" by King George lll.

The home had three bedrooms, a parlor, study room and keeping room. The latter room was an area located just off the kitchen of a home built during the Colonial era. It was used by a family to sleep in when the rest of the house was cold. Because the kitchen was always warm, the space often provided the only heated space in the house.

Both church congregations flourished during the next decade, and Beardsley oversaw services at the two locales. But when the American Revolution began, the minister found himself in harm's way.

Because Beardsley was a Tory and supported England, his presence in Poughkeepsie – a hotbed for patriots – became strained, especially after the British burned down Kingston, then the state capital. The situation became so intense that church services were suspended and Beardsley was ordered to remain on the farm except to visit the sick or baptize infants.

On Dec. 5, 1777, the local Council of Safety ordered Beardsley arrested as a Tory and directed that he and his family relocate to New York City, which was then controlled by British forces. They were allowed to take with them only their clothes, necessary bedding and provisions for their trip downriver.

In April 1778, Beardsley was appointed chaplain of the "Loyal American Regiment," a unit that engaged in battle against the Continental Army in the Hudson Valley, Pennsylvania and the Carolinas. Upon the fall of New York City in 1783, thousands of Loyalists, including the Beardsley family, fled to New Brunswick, Canada.

A few days after Beardsley departed Poughkeepsie, local merchant John Davis, who'd subscribed money for the glebe's construction, moved into the home. That began a long list of occupants and various uses of the property.

From 1780 to 1785 the Quartermaster offices of the Continental Army occupied the house. A second pastor was hired in 1787 and moved into Glebe House, but in 1791 when the Poughkeepsie church found it impossible to support his wages, he resigned his position and left.

The two congregations sold the property in 1792 to Peter DeReimer, who lived in the house until 1809. It is believed that the house was enlarged and extensively renovated during his ownership. In 1809, Trinity Church in Fishkill and Christ Church in Poughkeepsie decided to cease sharing a rector. Samuel Verplanck donated a farm in Stormville, East Fishkill, to Trinity Church to accommodate its minister with a glebe.

After DeReimer moved out, the property passed through a succession of owners with the original acreage gradually subdivided and sold off until 1868 when the house and only two acres of land on Main Street were sold to Michael Hoblich for use as a beer garden. Subsequent commercial uses of the house and property followed when two different florist shops and greenhouses occupied the house and grounds from 1896 through 1928.

When the latter of the two florist owners expressed her intention to demolish the house, the Poughkeepsie Common Council, Dutchess County Historical Society and Junior League of Poughkeepsie joined forces to rally in support of saving the structure. On April 1, 1929, the City of Poughkeepsie acquired its deed.

Following the home's complete restoration, the county's historical society and junior league staged occasional programs and other events at the Glebe House through January 2016, when its oversight shifted to the Mid-Hudson Heritage Center. That organization conducts tours, holds open house and presents various programs at the site. It still remains a city owned property.

To visit the historic site or to learn about upcoming programs and operating hours, call 845-485-8506.

Harmony Hall

Jacob Sloat was born in 1792, a grandson of Stephen Sloat, who had settled in what became the Village of Sloatsburg, Town of Ramapo, Rockland County, twenty-nine years earlier. The younger Sloat, who was described as a mechanical genius, established his first mill in the village in 1815, when he was twenty-three years old. The mill, which manufactured cotton twine, dominated the New York market, due in part to the arrival of the New York and Erie Railroad, which enabled Sloat to greatly expand his marketplace.

Sloat's reputation as an inventor, industrialist and entrepreneur grew through the years and, by the early 1850s, his mill was turning out as much as eight thousand pounds of twine every week. His inventions included the cap spindle and gimlet-pointed wood screw, which were a great benefit to his business. In 1813, Sloat laid claim to the third patent ever granted by the United States Patent Office.

Between his mill operation, business savvy and inventions, Sloat amassed considerable wealth and, in 1846, he designed and con-structed a three-story wood-frame mansion fronted on its east side by a sweeping lawn. Given its high vantage point, Sloat had a com-manding view of his mill operation that sat below.

Historians have long believed that Sloat himself – possibly with the assistance of his good friend and Hudson River School artist Jasper

Cropsey – designed the ornate mansion. While Cropsey was primarily known for his landscape artwork, he dabbled in architecture and drew up an early rendition of the Sloat mansion.

The structure took two years to complete and, when the family finally moved in, Sloat christened it Harmony Hall. The exterior of the large building was designed in a Greek Revival style although its interior space was a more a combination of Italianate and Picturesque styles, which was emerging as the preferred architectural style at the time Harmony Hall was constructed.

The exterior of the mansion was covered with pine clapboard and topped by a slightly pitched gabled roof. A veranda occupied the entire front of the structure's main floor. It was eventually enclosed by another owner to create additional rooms.

Inside, Sloat's overwhelming use of ornament and marble clearly reveals the heavy influence of Italian design. The L-shaped footprint of the overall mansion resulted when two wings were erected at the rear. All wall plaster and woodwork remains in place and of note are the twin fireplaces in the first-floor parlor that boast marble mantles.

The basement consists of three large, fully furnished rooms.

Sadly, Sloat did not enjoy his stately residence for long. When he died in 1857, it passed on to his wife of thirty-one years, Sarah. The couple's twenty-three-year-old son Henry purchased the mansion from his mother in 1861. In 1875, Henry married Carrie Schultz and started a family in the same home that he was brought up in.

Unfortunately, three years later, the high price of raw materials that was stimulated by the Civil War, was falling. Facing heavy competition from companies producing cheaper (albeit inferior) materials, the Sloatsburg Manufacturing Company started by Jacob Sloat at the beginning of the 19th century closed.

Following the death of Henry Sloat in 1905, the house passed on to his wife Carrie, who three years later sold it out of the family's ownership. The 20th century saw the residence go through various phases. It was an inn, then a restaurant and, finally, a nursing home. During this period, the home was modified considerably to meet each purpose.

After the state closed the nursing home down in 2003, it was placed on the local real estate market and recommended as an ideal site for the development of condominium housing. It was rescued by the Town of Ramapo in 2006, when officials purchased the historic property, then occupying two acres.

In 2007, the town acquired a grant from the New York State Office of Parks, Recreation and Historic Preservation to engage in a full restoration of the structure; the project was completed in 2015. While the town oversaw work on the mansion's exterior, the Friends of Harmony Hall, a group formed in 2007 and dedicated to the preservation of Jabob Sloat's historic home, restored the mansion's interior.

The Friends stage a number of musical and cultural events in the mansion. For more information, call the group at 845-712-5220. The mansion is located at 15 Liberty Rock Road, Sloatsburg.

Hill-Hold Farmstead

Hill-Hold, the home of prosperous farmer Thomas Bull, was built in 1769 on a large parcel of land in Campbell Hall, Town of Hamptonburgh, Orange County. Born in 1727, Bull was the fourth of twelve children born to William and Sarah Bull (see Bull Stone House chapter), who owned one hundred acres nearby.

In 1724, William Bull, who was extremely loyal to the Crown, petitioned King George 1 for additional land and was granted five hundred acres to add to his holdings. The now sizable property enabled William Bull to leave enough land to the second generation of his large family. Upon his death in 1755, he divided the property granted by the king to his third and fourth sons, William and Thomas.

The lot that Thomas acquired spans both sides of today's Route 416 and on its west side extends out right up to the Wallkill River.

In between planting and reaping crops, Thomas prepared to build a stately stone house reflective of the family's wealth. He cut the stones that would eventually be used in the home during breaks from farming. Paneling for the house was shipped from England and was eventually fitted into the two large first floor rooms, along with solid mahogany balls for the newels and mahogany balusters. The house also features wide plank floors and large fireplaces.

The two-story house is L-shaped in design. It was built of native limestone and features a slate gamble roof. On each end of the main block, a chimney protrudes through the roofline. When the house was finally completed, Thomas Bull and his wife moved in and – following the lead of his parents – the couple raised their own twelve children on the farm. And like his father, he was a staunch British loyalist, even during the American Revolution.

That position put him in a very precarious position in the Orange County community when he refused to sign the oath of allegiance to the state. During the Revolutionary War, he was imprisoned on several occasions. The fact that his wife was as strong a patriot as Thomas was a loyalist likely caused many spirited discussions in the household.

According to an account shared by a Bull descendent, one of the couple's sons, George, actually enlisted in the British army in the New England region. After the war ended, he relocated to Canada, never to return to the family farm.

A front porch was added to the house in 1850. During the 19th century, the structure became known as the Bull-Jackson Stone House because Civil War Captain William A. Jackson – the great-great grandson of Thomas Bull – was born in the house. The grounds include wood-frame outbuildings, which were likely erected through the 19th century.

After the last of the Bull descendants left the site in the 1960s, Orange County acquired the house and property. It now serves as the Hill-Hold Museum and is open to the public.

Visitors have a unique opportunity to experience what life was like on a Hudson Valley farm during the 1830s. Original furnishings featured in the museum include an old mahogany sideboard and hand-made items constructed by the Bull family's descendants. The grounds include a summer kitchen, a one-room schoolhouse, a smoke house, farm animals and a gift shop.

Hill-Hold Museum is located at 128 Route 416, Campbell Hall. Public tours of the house and grounds are provided for a modest fee on Friday, Saturday and Sunday, May through October, from 10 a.m.-4 p.m. Special events open to the public include a pumpkin festival, herb day, candlelight tours in December, Civil War reenactments and more. For more information, call the museum at 845-291-2404.

Adjacent to the museum and spanning 719 acres, the Thomas Bull Memorial Park is the second largest developed recreational area in Orange County. It was renamed in honor of Thomas Bull in 1965, when Bull's descendants donated 189 acres to the park.

Horace Greeley House

Horace Greeley was born Feb. 3, 1811, on a farm near Amherst, New Hampshire into a financially struggling family. He ran away from home at the age of fifteen and secured a printer's apprenticeship in East Poultney, Vermont, for the Northern Spectator. After the newspaper shut down in 1930, Greeley traveled to Erie, Pennsylvania, to rejoin his family, who had moved there.

While there he was hired by the Erie Gazette, and although he sought out a more prominent role in the newspaper industry, he remained in that job for two years to support his father. In late 1831, Greeley moved to New York City with the hope of fulfilling his dreams. While finding employment at a mainstream publication proved difficult, Greeley was able to set up his own print shop and, in 1833, began to publish the Constitutionalist, which came out three times a week.

In 1834, he published the first issue of The New Yorker in partnership with Jonas Winchester. While the publication attracted a huge readership, the Panic of 1837 caused it to close. Greeley also published a campaign news sheet for the new Whig Party during the 1834 campaign.

Greeley met Mary Young Cheney, a teacher, shortly after moving to New York. She relocated south to secure a teaching position and, on July 5, 1836, the couple married in Warrenton, North Carolina. Greeley kept working on behalf of the Whig Party and freelanced with numerous supporting newspapers, most prominently in 1838, when he became the editor of the Jeffersonian and then the Log Cabin.

By the end of the 1840 campaign, Log Cabin had secured a circulation of eighty thousand, which led Greeley to establish a daily newspaper called the New York Tribune. Greeley's interest in politics was almost equal to his publishing interests and when David Jackson was unseated as congressman of New York's sixth district in 1848 for election fraud, Greeley was selected to finish his term. In 1872, he was a candidate for U.S. President against Ulysses S. Grant. He lost the election by a wide margin.

In 1853, with railroad service available in the Town of Chappaqua, Westchester County, Greeley purchased a seventy-eight-acre farm south of village center that was originally intended to be the family's summer home. He went on to build a home on a wooded hillside that became known as the House in the Woods. However, his wife found it too remote and shady.

Greeley purchased another house along the main thoroughfare in 1864 that had been built in 1820 by a local farmer named Haviland. It was a simple side-hall house, which Greeley expanded considerably after moving in.

The new interior layout in the addition included a large room in front and a smaller room to the rear on both floors. The original stairways were removed and replaced by stairways that sat between the two rooms, rising from the ground floor up two stories to the second level.

A kitchen was on the ground floor while the first floor included a formal parlor, dining room, pantry and music room. Its second floor featured a master bedroom, a smaller bedroom for the Greeley's two daughters, a family parlor and a bedroom for the family's maid. The Greeley clan spent summers in the house until 1872, when both Mary and then Horace Greeley died. He had just completed his run for president.

The Greeley daughters – Ida and Gabrielle – returned to the house in summer 1873 with an older cousin, Cecilia Cleveland. But following that stay, both siblings moved into what is known as Hillside House. Gabrielle retained possession of the house, along with the nearby farm. In 1875, the House in the Woods was destroyed by fire.

Gabrielle began to rent the village house out until she finally sold it in 1926. During the 1930s, the house fell into a state of disrepair. Two local citizens saved it from being torn down by restoring the structure and converting the first floor into the Greeley House Gift Shop. A restaurant was also operated briefly in the ground-floor kitchen.

The house was sold in 1959 and its new owners enlarged the gift shop to occupy the entire dwelling. In 1998, following the gift shop's closure, the New Castle Historical Society purchased the Greeley house, restored it to its original appearance and, in 2000, opened it to the public as a museum

Located at 100 King St., Chappaqua, the museum is open Tuesdays through Thursdays and Saturdays from 1-4 p.m. or by appointment. Special events such as a Victorian Valentine's Tea, Holiday Crafts and Tree Lighting and more are held at the house every year. A collection of artifacts including the desk that Horace Greeley used at his New York Tribune office are on display.

For more information, call the New Castle Historical Society at 914-238-4666.

still features a steeply pitched roof shingled in cedar shake with board and batten siding. It occupies a one-acre parcel of land directly across from the Amenia Rural Cemetery.

The schoolhouse's interior holds the remains of the woodstove and flue and the lower section of a brick chimney. Like many one-room schoolhouses of that era, the building has two entrances, one each for boys and girls. When the town began to consolidate classes into a more centralized school system during the late 1920s, Indian Rock Schoolhouse closed in 1927. It remained vacant for decades.

During the 1950s, farmers used the building as a storage facility. Barn doors were added to the rear of the building to allow easier access.

In 2001, a group of volunteers from the community with a desire to save the historic structure acquired the property and building. Its ownership was then transferred to the Webutuck Country Schoolhouse Association of Maplebrook School. While many of the former one-room schoolhouses in Amenia were converted through the years to single- family residences, the association raised funds to restore the Indian Rock structure to its original appearance.

Some who volunteered to do a complete restoration of the schoolhouse – and who were well-versed in the construction of vintage buildings – claimed that based on the way the wooden pins were affixed in the attic, the building was originally constructed between 1790 and 1820.

The schoolhouse is now used for Maplebrook students' community service projects as well as for hosting programs for area schools and staging town celebrations. It provides visitors with a unique opportunity to experience an early environment for education in the region.

The goal of the group was to maintain the building, to provide programs about local history there and to enable history buffs and others to visit it in order to gain a better understanding of the schooling process before central school systems were created.

During warm months, the schoolhouse committee stages a variety of events there, including old-fashioned games of skill. During the school year, students get to spend time at the schoolhouse to experi-ence first-hand what it was like to be taught in that environment.

A popular Arbor Day picnic is held and Summer Sundays feature educational and fun programs during July. Indian Rock School-house is located at 25 Mygatt Road, north of town center and east of Routes 22/44 and Old North Road. To arrange a group visit, call Ann Linden at 845-373-8338.

Innisfree Garden

Tucked away at 362 Tyrell Road, one mile south of Route 44 in Millbrook, Innisfree Garden is 185 acres of streams, waterfalls, terraces, retaining walls, rocks, and plants, based on the principles of Chinese landscape design. Originally the country estate of Walter and Marion Beck, in accordance with their wills the grounds became a public garden in 1960.

Its name was derived from the 1888 poem "The Lake Isle of Innisfree" by Irish poet William Yeats.

Avid gardener and heiress Marion Beck began to amass what became a 924-acre tract of land prior to her marriage in 1922 to Walter Beck. Beck was a teacher and artist who was influenced by Asian art and, during the 1930s, he became infatuated with Chinese and Japanese garden designs.

That passion began a decades-long initiative to develop the grounds at Innisfree. Having admired the work of 8th-century Chinese poet, painter, and gardener Wang Wei, Beck attempted to replicate similar designs on his Millbrook estate. Wei's garden, Wangchuan Villa, was a creation of focused gardens and garden vignettes within a larger landscape based on naturalism.

In 1938, the Becks met Harvard graduate student Lester Collins, who would become a renowned landscape architect. Over time, Col-

Jacob T. Walden House

A 1½-story, three by two-bay house that dates to around 1768 in today's Village of Walden, Orange County, was built by Samuel Erwin. Erwin likely purchased the land the house sits on from Edward Gatehouse, its original patentee.

Set on a rubble stone foundation, the side-hall house was constructed of cut stone and featured a gambrel roof that consisted of wood shingles. The walls in the house are two-feet thick. Its interior features a living room, keeping room, and dining room on its first level, with two bedrooms on the second floor.

Jacob T. Walden was a successful New York City merchant who first came to Kidd Town, as the community was then known, in 1812. The town's original name was in honor of Alexander Kidd and his family, who settled in the area in 1736. It was the fast moving Wallkill River in the community that captured Walden's attention and entrepreneurial spirit.

Walden liquidated his business concerns in New York City and established a business in Orange County by purchasing property with water rights to the river. He initially purchased the Kidd Mill at the foot of the falls and attempted to try his hand at the manufacture of cotton fabric.

Walden purchased his house from Samuel Erwin's son William, the same year he arrived in town. He named it Old Hearthstone. He went on to create a number of flourishing industrial ventures along the river, including a wool mill near his cotton mill.

During the late 19th century, the river provided power for the New York and Walden Knife Company, a business that was so successful that it flourished well into the 20th century. The operation became internationally known for its superior and finely crafted products.

Visitors enter the house through its Dutch double doors (original to the house, along with its side-lights), then enter the side hall, which is large enough to welcome guests. Immediately behind the stair hall is a corner working fireplace in the first-floor keeping room, one of three fireplaces on the floor set triangularly back to back. A large piece of furniture in the room once belonged to the Van Wyck family of New Hurley and was used to store blankets, linens and other items.

The staircase leading to upstairs bedrooms is original to the house. The living room boasts a wing chair, Federal style convex mirror and a slant-top desk that is signed by Thomas Burling, a cabinet maker who trained under Samuel Prince. Burling was thought to be the most skilled furniture maker in the country and produced fine pieces for both George Washington and Thomas Jefferson.

The dining room furniture is of the Empire Period. A distinguishing feature from that time period can be observed on a sideboard where the use of animal paw designs on the legs of the furniture and animal heads with nose rings serve as drawer pulls.

The larger of the two bedrooms on the second level also features Empire Period furniture, including a sleigh bed and matching bureau while the second bedroom boasts a maple four-post bed that dates to the 1790s.

Jacob Walden eventually moved back to New York City, where he died in 1855. That same year, due to the various businesses that he established and his determination to create a thriving industry in the Orange County community, the village's name was changed from Kidd Town to Walden, New York.

Walden's daughter maintained residency for some time in the Hudson Valley house but it was ultimately sold out of family ownership.

A few owners followed and, at one point, the house was divided into two apartments. As time passed, the house fell into a serious state of disrepair.

Between the house's condition and plans to establish a gas station right next door, a group of concerned citizens in Walden formed the Historical Society of Walden and Wallkill Valley during the 1950s. Its primary objective was to save the historic house.

Society members worked tirelessly to repair and restore the house to its original appearance when Walden lived there. The group continues to meet at the house on the third Wednesday of the month, in spring and fall. Meetings are open to the public.

To learn more about special events and functions staged at the Walden House by the society, visit www.thewaldenhouse.org. The Jacob T. Walden House is located at 30 N. Montgomery St., Walden.

Jasper Cropsey House and Studio

Courtesy of Newington-Cropsey Foundation

Perched on a hillside with enviable views of the Hudson River along Washington Avenue in Hastings-on-Hudson, Westchester County, sits a house that was the residence of Jasper Cropsey, a significant painter of the Hudson River School during the 19th century. Designed in part by Cropsey, who had architectural training, the wood frame, three-bay by one-bay 1½-story house features a one-story porch on its front (west) façade.

It was built in 1835 and purchased by Cropsey fifty years later as his final residence. He named it Ever Rest.

Born on Feb. 18, 1823, on his family's farm in Rossville, Staten Island, Cropsey displayed an early passion for art. In the late 1830s when he was fourteen years old, he secured a five-year apprenticeship at the architectural office of John Trench in New York City. He founded his own company in 1843 and began to create watercolors and oil paintings at the National Academy of Design.

Cropsey first exhibited his work at the academy in 1844, and one year later he was elected an associate member. He gave up all other ventures in favor of landscape painting. He would, however, design buildings of note for friends throughout his career.

Soon, his landscape paintings gained him fame and fortune in

America and England. His style reflected similar compositions of Thomas Cole of Catskill, founder of the Hudson River School and Cropsey's idol. Cropsey's work became known for his lavish use of color, and his admirers embraced his fall landscape scenes, which were distinctive for their bold and striking presentation.

Married to Maria Cooley in May 1847, the couple traveled to Europe for two years, visiting Italy, France, Switzerland and England. Upon returning home, he opened a studio in New York and continued to churn out work that displayed his unique and well-known characteristics.

In 1869, Cropsey designed and built a twenty-nine-room board and batten mansion and art studio in Warwick. He christened it Aladdin. He continued to maintain a residence in New York City but, by the mid-1870s, his style and those of the Hudson River School in general were falling out of fashion.

In 1884, with his paintings failing to command the high prices of earlier work, Cropsey's Aladdin was sold and many paintings, furniture and other possession were auctioned off. Cropsey moved across the river to Hastings-on-Hudson. After initially renting a house, he purchased the home on Washington Avenue in 1885. The house was originally built in 1835 in a carpenter gothic style by local industrialist William Saunders.

Cropsey enlarged the house, adding an art studio that was very similar to the one he designed at his Warwick estate. It featured a large windowed cupola and full-length window facing north to let in as much natural light as possible. After he moved to Hastings-on-Hudson, Cropsey's work was limited to local scenes.

Cropsey and his wife lived out their lives at Ever Rest. He died at the home in 1900, at the age of seventy-seven. His wife Maria died six years later.

Ever Rest was left to Cropsey's great-granddaughter Isabel. Aladdin was tragically destroyed by fire in 1909. The remaining paintings at the Ever Rest home were sold at auction through Silo Art Galleries in Manhattan to settle Cropsey's estate. Isabel and her husband William Steinschneider moved into the home and were the last family members to reside there. Steinschneider died in 1970.

In 1977, the Newington-Cropsey Foundation was founded by Cropsey's great-great granddaughter, Barbara Newington, with the objective of preserving and displaying the home and paintings of Jasper F. Cropsey. The structure was added to the National Register of Historic Places in the early 1970s.

In 1994, the Gallery of Art was built near the home to enable the foundation to exhibit more of the collection of Cropsey's paintings. It also has space for temporary and traveling exhibits. Designed in the Gothic Revival style and boasting thirty-foot ceilings, the gallery was opened to the public on Oct. 16, 1994. Accessed from the rotunda, the space features ornate woodwork and a terrazzo floor. A large number of Cropsey's oil paintings are on display there.

Paintings on display at Ever Rest are part of a permanent collection, accumulated through the years by Barbara Newington and the foundation. Free guided tours are offered at Ever Rest and at the Gallery of Art.

Ever Rest is located at 49 Washington Ave., Hastings-on-Hudson. Tours for groups or individuals are offered from 10 a.m.-1 p.m., Monday through Friday. The Gallery of Art is at 25 Cropsey Lane. Tours are available from 1-5 p.m. Tours at both sites are by appointment only and should be scheduled at least one week in advance. Groups are limited to fifteen people unless special arrangements are made in advance.

Call 914-478-7990 for additional information or to arrange a tour.

boasted sixty rooms, with its main block standing 2½ stories. Its exterior was fitted with a tall square tower on its southeast corner, a hexagonal tower on the northeast and a round tower on the northwest. Leland appropriately named it Castleview.

Spanning 130 feet long and 88 feet deep with an exterior that consisted of quarried grey granite, its first-floor ceilings were sixteen feet high while the second level featured fourteen-foot high ceilings. The mansion became known for its frescos (oil paint applied directly on plaster) painted by several artists depicting colorful scenes of both national history and mystical subjects.

While the artwork was at some point painted over, the home's elegance is still found in its quality woodwork, blue and gold Minton tiled floor in the front hallway, and three original fireplaces. The pitched and domed roof over the third floor was partially masked by dormers, gables and turrets, which enhanced its castle-like design.

Leland enjoyed hosting various functions at his home, and invited guests entered the house through two tall, black walnut doors, each of which featured a lion's head flanked by slender sidelights crowned with Gothic details.

Having developed a strong attraction for the property surrounding his estate, Leland purchased David's Island in Echo Bay in 1861 with the intention of building a hotel there. The area was well suited to attract well-to-do tourists to a luxury resort on the sound.

Sadly, that year the nation faced serious challenges when the Civil War broke out. Leland ended up leasing the island to the Union Army for use as a military hospital. When the war ended, he sold the island to the government and it eventually was transformed into Fort Slocum.

In Saratoga, the family did well, hosting many Union Army generals and other leaders of industry and finance at the Union Hotel. Originally named Union Hall, the siblings changed it to the Grand Union Hotel in 1869. Unfortunately, the Lelands over-spent on alterations and construction of other buildings, including an opera house. The cost proved prohibitive and the family filed for bankruptcy in February 1872.

That same year, Simeon Leland was forced to retire when his lease on the Metropolitan Hotel expired and was conveyed to William A. "Boss" Tweed, an American politician most famous for being the "boss" of Tammany Hall. That was the Democratic Party political machine that played a major role in the politics of New York City and the state during the 19th century.

Leland died later that year deeply in debt. His mansion in New Rochelle eventually went into foreclosure. Its new owner, the Manhattan Life Insurance Company, allowed Mrs. Leland and her children to live in the castle through 1880, at which time it was leased to the Queens County Hunt Club. For two years, the club used it as a lodging facility under the name Castle Inn.

In 1884, Adrian Iselin Jr. purchased the castle and its surrounding property for the purpose of developing it. Soon after, Residence Park was established as one of the first planned residential parks and communities in the United States. Leland's original forty-acre estate was reduced to the mansion on a two-and-a-half acre parcel.

The castle itself went on to house the New Collegiate Institute, a boarding school for boys, from 1889 to 1892; it later became Miss Moore's Academy for young ladies. A massive fire in a chimney in 1897 caused considerable damage to the roof and part of the second floor. Without insurance, Miss Moore left the castle

After Iselin promised to repair the damage, it was purchased by Mother Irene Gill for use as the Ursuline Seminary. In 1902, a large wing was built onto the north side of the building, the attic rooms were subdivided, and one of the former second floor bedrooms was converted into a small chapel. Leland Castle eventually became part of the College of New Rochelle and today houses its administrative offices. It is located at 29 Castle Place, New Rochelle.

Lewis Tompkins Hose Company

In 1886, Lewis Tompkins, owner of one of Beacon's most suc-cessful hat manufacturing companies, established a firefighting company on lower Main Street in the Village of Fishkill Landing (now City of Beacon). Because Tompkins's Dutchess Hat Works as well as another hat company owned by his brother had suffered considerable damage as a result of several fires, he had the firehouse built close to the family businesses.

Until that time, lower Main Street in the village did not have an organized fire company. To honor its benefactor, the new outfit was christened the Tompkins Hose Company.

The village board had acquired property on Main Street, just east of today's Wolcott Avenue (Route 9D) to make space for the new firehouse. The two-story Second Empire-style structure was de-signed by architects Schuyler Tillman and Benjamin Hall and its construction was completed in 1893. A third floor was added to the building in later years.

At the outset, the fire company used a hand-drawn hose cart, which meant firefighters had to manually pull it to the scene of a fire. That lasted for eleven years until the heavy and cumbersome cart was replaced with a horse-drawn wagon.

Once that equipment was placed into service, Fishkill Landing had the distinction of having the only fire company in the region with its own fire horse. Housed in a stable that occupied a portion of the firehouse's first floor, the horse – Ben – became a familiar and beloved part of the community.

While the Tompkins Hose Company owned and cared for Ben, other fire companies in the area had to rely on borrowed horses from local stables when the need arose. By having Ben in-house, the Tompkins Hose Company was able to get to the scene of a fire more quickly.

Ben remained a valued member of the company until he was retired in 1918, when the department acquired a shiny red Ahrens-Fox motorized fire engine. Ben was rewarded for years of dedicated service with a quiet retirement at a stable in nearby Glenham, where he is now buried.

The members of the all-volunteer Tompkins Hose Company demonstrated an unwavering dedication to their purpose and tasks. They were known to immediately stop whatever they were doing and race to the scene of a fire upon hearing the alarm sound. Sadly, while battling one particular blaze in 1955 and attempting to save a child from a burning building, J. Robert Cramer perished in the line of duty.

Cramer was the president of Tompkins Hose Company at the time of his death. To date, he remains the only firefighter in Beacon history to have died while battling a fire.

In addition to the valuable service rendered to Fishkill Landing, members of Tompkins Hose regularly participated in village celebrations and parades. Like other local fire companies of the era, it also boasted its own baseball team.

One member of the Tompkins team, Elmer Steele, dazzled opposing teams during the early 1900s with his enviable pitching skills. So advanced was his raw talent that, in 1907, Steele was drafted into baseball's major leagues, enjoying a career pitching for the Boston Red Sox, Pittsburgh Pirates and Brooklyn Robins (later to become the Dodgers).

In 1982, when the fire company outgrew its Main Street building, it moved to a new facility at 13 South Ave. The original Tompkins

Hose Company firehouse, which stands at 162 Main St., is now occupied by Hudson Beach Glass, a glass gallery and studio.

Montgomery/Livingston House

The 18th-century Colonial-style clapboard home at 77 Livingston St. in the Village of Rhinebeck, Dutchess County, has served as the Daughters of the American Revolution (DAR) Chancellor Livingston Chapter House since 1930. It was presented to the chapter by its founding member and first regent, Helen Reed de Laporte, who had purchased the home two years earlier.

The structure is famous for having been the residence of Janet Livingston and General Richard Montgomery from the day they were married in 1773 through 1775, when he became the first Continental Army officer to be killed during the Revolutionary War.

Jude Henry Beekman was granted a patent by the Crown in 1703 that consisted of most of the land in today's Rhinebeck. Upon the marriage of his granddaughter, Janet Livingston, he offered her and her husband, General Montgomery, the use of the modest house while their estate, Grasmere, was being built just south of the village.

The house was then located on the Old Post Road, on a parcel of land at today's 88 Montgomery Street (Rt. 9). In the spring of 1775, Richard Montgomery was offered the commission of Major-General in the Continental Army. Having accepted the commission, he and General Philip Schuyler were placed in command of the Northern Forces.

Their goal was to drive the British army out of Canada, but Montgomery was killed in battle while attempting to capture the walled city of Quebec, Canada, on Dec. 31, 1775.

Following Montgomery's death, the devastated widow Livingston was determined to oversee the completion of Grasmere in tribute to her late husband. She lived in the mansion until 1802 when it became increasingly difficult for her to stay there without Montgomery.

She built a new home, Chateau de Montgomery (today's Montgomery Place) farther north in Barrytown and moved there.

When Thomas Edgerley, editor of the Rhinebeck Gazette, purchased the original Montgomery Street home in 1867 and decided to replace it with a grander structure, he realized the historic significance of it. Rather than demolishing it, he decided to relocate it to nearby Academy Street (today's Livingston Street).

The house was transported the six blocks by cutting down a number of large trees, smoothing off the rough bark and placing them beside the house. The house was then lifted off its foundation and placed atop the rounded logs. The house was dragged the entire distance by oxen with the assistance of a team of horses. Several men, positioned at the rear of the house, would collect each log as it rolled out the back of the structure, then reposition it in front of the approaching house. This kept the house rolling forward.

Helen de Laporte founded the Rhinebeck DAR chapter in 1917. It was named in honor of Robert Livingston, Janet Livingston's brother. As chancellor of New York State, he administered the oath of office to George Washington when he became the nation's first president.

In 1928, de Laporte purchased the former Montgomery/Livingston house. The four-column Victorian porch that originally fronted the home deteriorated considerably over time and was eventually removed. It was replaced with a smaller porch, which remains there today.

In the absence of a DAR Chapter House at that time, de Laporte presented the deed for her home to the group to fill that void during a 1930 meeting held at the nearby Beekman Arms. It has since been the site of monthly meetings for chapter members.

The house now displays museum artifacts in the west room of the first floor. There are exhibits about Richard Montgomery and Janet Livingston, along with temporary exhibits such as a recent Civil War display.

A second-floor room is dedicated to Helen de Laporte. Very active as the community's former historian, de Laporte was instrumental in documenting many of the historic buildings in Rhinebeck. It was through her effort and determination that, in 1918, she hired professional photographer Harry Coutant to capture many images of the surrounding neighborhood on glass plate negatives.

The Chapter House is open to the public June through late August on Saturdays from 1-4 p.m. or by appointment. The Montgomery/ Livingston house is located at 77 Livingston St., Rhinebeck. For more information about the DAR Chancellor Livingston Chapter or to arrange a visit, call 845-871-1777.

New Hamburg Train Tunnel

While hardly noticeable during summer months when leaves and brush obstruct its opening, there is a long abandoned 19th-century railroad tunnel just east of tracks in New Hamburg, a hamlet in the southern corner of the Town of Poughkeepsie, Dutchess County. Built in 1849, it is located just beyond the northeast section of the hamlet's Metro-North station parking lot behind a security gate.

When rail service arrived in the mid-Hudson Valley region during the mid-1800s, the tunnel served the Hudson River Railroad's New York City to Albany line.

Of the eight tunnels that were built along the newly introduced rail line, the one in New Hamburg has the distinction of being the longest, at 1,400 feet. It took the combined effort of four hundred workers, nine blacksmith shops, twelve thousand pounds of steel drills and tools and six thousand kegs of blasting powder to create the eighteen-foot tall, twenty-eight-foot wide tunnel.

Two shafts, one of which still exists, were carved into the top of the rock to allow much of the tunnel's excavation to be drawn up through them by steam power. The rock itself was so hard that brick lining was not needed – something normally required when building the tunnel's arch to prevent loose stones from falling onto the tracks.

Because train service was introduced before the New Hamburg tunnel was complete, passengers traveling north and south were originally required to disembark the train before entering the hamlet, where they would be carried by a small boat around the community to board another train that sat waiting on the other side of the tunnel.

Passengers traveling north disembarked in an area that was known as Old Troy, just south of the mouth of the Wappinger Creek. There they boarded the waiting water vessel to carry them the short distance north.

When the tunnel was finally completed in 1851, a complex was established adjacent to it that included a wood frame passenger station, a freight depot and a gatekeeper's shack. The passenger station sat at Main Street (which at the time extended across the tracks) in the vicinity of today's Metro-North parking lot entrance.

When a train approached the hamlet, the gatekeeper routinely came out of the shack and lowered the Main Street barriers by hand to stop traffic.

In 1871, New Hamburg was the site of a major railroad tragedy. On the frigid night of Feb. 6, a twenty-five-car freight train known as Extra Number Three departed Greenbush, a suburb of Albany, southbound along the Hudson River Railroad line. Because the train's iron wheels became brittle in bitter cold, its brakes and axles were inspected before the train began its journey.

Coupled with the fact that the train was hauling oil-filled tank cars, that night's run was filled with uncertainty despite the fact that the train's conductor, Edgar Underwood, was experienced in his job. In fact, Underwood would fail to adhere to a new safety procedure that called for him to string a bell rope through the cars to alert the engineer of an emergency.

Meanwhile, at the 30th Street Depot in New York City, the Second Pacific Express was six minutes late leaving for Albany, Buffalo and points west. The railroad superintendent advised its engineer to use caution and to avoid trying to make up lost time due to the weather. As it traveled northbound along the route, it actually lost additional time.

At 10:17 p.m., as the freight train exited the tunnel just north of the

New Hamburg station, Dan Carroll, the station switchman, observed sparks emanating from beneath an oil car in the middle of the train. Determining that a broken axle was causing the sparks, Carroll attempted to alert the middle brakeman – Underwood's brother, Charles – who was in the caboose to stay warm.

When the damaged car passed over the switch just south of the station, the axle disengaged, causing the train to bounce. Without the warning bell rope, none of the crew could alert the engineer to stop the train.

As the train neared the drawbridge over the Wappinger Creek, the damaged car struck a bridge piling. It tore away from the car in front and flipped over, coming to rest at an angle across the northbound track.

The engineer finally stopped the train. He was aware that a northbound train would be arriving at the location soon, so he grabbed a red light and instructed a flagman in the nearby tower to join him running south along the tracks to signal the danger ahead.

As its passengers on the northbound train began to settle in for the night, the engineer of the Second Pacific Express noticed what appeared to be two faint red lights and a bright white light ahead. He signaled the brakeman to engage the patent brakes. The brakes didn't hold because they were designed for coaches, not large sleeper cars. In desperation, the engineer threw the train into reverse.

It didn't work. The northbound train crashed into the disabled tank car that sat in its path, causing an explosion. As the northbound train lay on its side on the bridge, all of the oil tank cars and the bridge itself were engulfed in flames.

Within seconds, the burning bridge collapsed, sending a number of the damaged train cars into the icy waters below. The William T. Garner Engine Company from Wappingers Falls responded quickly, and a work train fitted with a crane was dispatched from Poughkeepsie. As shocked nearby residents took in survivors, others began to recover bodies.

In all, twenty-two people died. The incident received coverage in newspapers across the country. It was one of the worst tragedies to occur in Dutchess County history.

As years passed and train travel flourished nationwide, railroad officials saw a need for increased service along the Hudson River line. Workers blasted away a rock ledge that sat just west of the New Hamburg tunnel and began to install two additional sets of tracks. Farther north along the line the additional sets of tracks meant the removal of stations in Hyde Park and Staatsburg. New brick stations were built farther east.

In 1930, the New Hamburg railroad operation went through a dramatic change when the new sets of tracks were added. The railroad kept expanding train traffic along the line and eventually they used four sets of tracks. But rather than try to enlarge the New Hamburg tunnel to accommodate the additional set of tracks, they just built around it.

The passenger platform and an underpass that still exist at the site were built to allow safe passage from the parking lot. Two roads – Bridge Street and Reed Road – were also built, the latter actually passing over the tunnel.

At that point, Main Street was divided. Its eastern spur became the entrance to today's parking lot and its western portion extended to the river. The tunnel remained in use throughout the construction projects to maintain rail service on the line.

Today, the fourteen hundred-foot underground span stands unobstructed but there is no interior lighting.

Old Drovers Inn

Old Drovers Inn in Dover Plains, a hamlet in the Town of Dover, Dutchess County, is the last standing lodging and dining establishment that once existed along a route that, during the 19th century, was known as "the great road from New York City to Vermont." Its location at the intersection of East Duncan Road and Old Post Road (County Route 6) was a major thoroughfare for cowboys who drove herds of cattle from more northern states to New York City.

The heavy livestock traffic led to the establishment of inns to provide rest stops for weary drovers.

The eleven acres that the structure presently occupies was part of a larger parcel owned by Ebenezer Preston, who settled there in 1727. Originally built as a farmhouse, it became known as Clear Water Inn when the business was established, then later as Preston's Inn. Ebenezer and his brother John eventually changed the name to Old Drovers Inn. The lodging and dining facility quickly attracted cattle drovers – a group of professional middle men who purchased herds of cattle and swine from New England farmers and then drove them down to markets in New York City to sell them at a decent profit.

After the rigors of working on long, dusty trails every day, the cowboys enjoyed the opportunity to relax and drink rum during evening hours. And because they always had ready cash on hand as a result

Old Southeast Church

Sitting on a hillside adjacent to Route 22 in the Town of Southeast, near Brewster, Putnam County, is a two-story, four-bay by three-bay house of worship that was built in 1793-94. It was the last of three churches built in the town beginning in 1735 when Elisha Kent relocated to the area after leaving his congregational church in Newtown, Connecticut.

The first meeting house, located along Dykemans Road, was a log-frame building. Kent replaced the structure with another edifice in 1761 that sat close to the Old Southeast Church's location in the hamlet of Doansburg, then a principle locale in the county. The new location was likely selected because it was close to Kent's home and farm.

Kent eventually left the parish to establish a new church closer to Carmel, where he died in 1776 at the age of seventy-five. He was interred at the Old Southeast Cemetery on Route 22 next to his first wife, Abigail Moss Kent, who predeceased him by twenty-five years. Hers is the oldest marked grave in Putnam County.

In 1793, the congregation in Southeast voted to build a larger edifice near the location of the 1761 church. A committee that consisted of David L. De Forest, Joseph Crane Jr. and John Waring was tasked with moving the project forward and, in June 1794, the Old Southeast Church was completed at a cost of £750.

The committee oversaw, not only the construction of the new fifty-foot by thirty-eight-foot building but also its exterior painting, lath and plaster work, along with interior touches such as new pew doors, a pulpit and stairs. The interior was also white washed and wood surfaces were polished.

On March 5, 1830, the church suffered fire damage, which led to alterations in addition to repairs. The building's front doors were moved from the south side to the west end of the church, a belfry was added to its exterior, the interior balcony was reoriented and a vestibule was added. The exterior clapboards still in place today date to the 1830 makeover.

The total cost for the 1830 alterations and repairs came to $1,115. The church organ is a Mason and Hamlin Reed Pump model, built around 1875. It contains three sets of reeds and ten stops.

The church did not undergo any changes during the 20th century and still lights its interior space with the same fixtures that were installed in the late 19th century.

The congregation flourished at Old Southeast Church through the mid-19th century, when the arrival of the New York Central Railroad's Harlem Line a bit west in Brewster stimulated both population growth and industry farther south.

In 1854, a new Presbyterian Church was built in Southeast Center (Sodom) and in 1886 the Brewster Presbyterian Church opened in the Village of Brewster, resulting in a sharp decline in the congregation at Old Southeast Church. After 1966, the building was unused and, over time, showed signs of deterioration. In 1969, the historic building became the focus of attention for the Landmarks Preservation Committee of the Southeast Museum, which purchased the structure in 1977.

An intense fundraising campaign raised money for several restoration projects: a new roof, complete painting of the church's interior and exterior, and the repair of its large windows. Today, the Old Southeast Church is the oldest house of worship in Putnam County.

Just west of the Old Southeast Church stands the Doanesburg Schoolhouse, which was built in the first half of the 19th century and served students through its closure in 1947 when centralized school districts were introduced. The one-story, three-bay by one-bay building is the oldest unaltered schoolhouse in the county. Inside the one-room schoolhouse, one teacher taught up to sixteen children from kindergarten to eighth grade.

The building was purchased by the Landmarks Preservation Committee in 1978. Today, school children visit the old schoolhouse to better understand the methods of teaching in earlier times.

The committee also oversees a third historic site in town, the Walter Brewster House, which was built in 1850. Two years prior to building the house, Brewster and his brother James purchased a 134-acre farm that eventually became the Village of Brewster. They built passenger and freight railroad stations, which were appropriately dubbed Brewster's Station.

Brewster's home is a fine example of Greek Revival-style architecture and, in the late 19th century, it became home to John Gail Borden, who managed the Borden's Milk Factory nearby. The stately structure went through various uses in later years, serving as an apartment building, home for the Knights of Columbus and a temporary school while the senior high school in town was being built.

Now fully restored by the committee, its interior furnishings, donated by local citizens, are not original to the house but are accurate for the period. The Landmarks Preservation Committee rents the Walter Brewster House and Old Southeast Church for meetings, weddings, receptions and cocktail parties.

The Walter Brewster house is located at 43 Oak St., Brewster. For more information or to arrange a tour, call the Landmarks Preservation Committee at 845-279-7429.

Patriot's Park

Foot bridges allow visitors to cross Andre's Brook, the boundary line between Tarrytown and Sleepy Hollow.

On Sept. 20, 1780, British Major John Andre traveled north along the Hudson River on the sloop Vulture to meet with American General Benedict Arnold, then commander of West Point. Their meeting was to discuss terms of Arnold's surrendering the fort to the British in return for £20,000.

On Sept. 22, the Vulture came under fire from Continental Army troops that were guarding Verplanck's Point and was forced to retreat down river without Andre back aboard. The British major was forced to dress in civilian clothes and ride a horse back toward British lines with a passport identifying him as John Anderson. The clothes and passport were provided by Arnold. In Andre's boot were instructions written in Arnold's hand that outlined how the British should take the fort.

On the morning of Sept. 23, as Andre approached Tarrytown, he was challenged by militiamen John Paulding, Isaac Van Wart and David Williams. Because one of the men was wearing a Hessian soldier's overcoat, Andre mistook them for Tories and explained that he was a British officer. He was taken prisoner and, while searching his boots, the treasonous papers were discovered.

The men turned down Andre's bribe of his horse and a watch to let him go and Paulding accompanied him to the Continental Army's headquarters nearby. After being initially detained in North Castle, Andre was transported across the Hudson River, where he was imprisoned at the '76 House inn and tavern in Tappan, the one and only time the building was used as a military prison.

Andre was tried and found guilty as being a spy at the Old Dutch Church in Tappan. He was hanged on Oct. 2, 1780. If the devious plan of Arnold and Andre had succeeded and the British took over West Point, they would have accomplished a primary objective of cutting off New England from the rest of the colonies.

In 1853, a monument was erected about two hundred yards west of the site of Andre's capture. It is one of the earliest tributes in the nation related to the American Revolution. To commemorate the centennial of Andre's capture, the monument was redesigned in 1880 and was included in a residential plan called Brookside Park, designed by the architectural firm Carrere and Hastings. Approximately seventy thousand people attended the rededication ceremony.

The firm was commissioned to design eight houses on the grounds, which would be leased by the property's owner, Eugene Jones, with the surrounding land serving as a residential park. Jones sold the parcel to Amos Clark in 1896. In 1911, the Knox School for Girls purchased it. A subsequent owner, the Highland Manor School for Girls, operated there from 1920 to 1942.

Following the school's closure, the structures on the grounds fell into severe disrepair and the property was sold to Worcester Warner and Victor Spanberg, who donated it to the villages of Tarrytown and North Tarrytown (Sleepy Hollow, since 1996). Seven of the eight structures were demolished and the parcel was renamed Patriot's Park.

During the 1940s, a local garden club was formed to improve and maintain the grounds. The foundations of the razed buildings were filled in and graded and walking paths were created throughout the park. The last of the houses standing on the grounds was torn down in 1970. A waterway named Andre's Brook runs through the park and serves as the boundary line between the two villages.

Located south of the brook at the park's entrance and behind an iron fence is the Captors' Monument. It features a bronze statue of John Paulding, one of the three men who had captured Andre. A gatehouse, the only surviving structure from the grounds' days as Brookside Park, stands north of the brook. Three stone bridges add to the ambiance.

Visitors are welcome to walk the four-acre grounds and reflect on the importance of the action taken here in 1780, which had a profound effect on the Continental Army's ability to maintain control of the Hudson Valley region.

Patriot's Park is located at 121 N. Broadway on the west side of Route 9.

Potash House

The one-story fieldstone building built around 1760 on Quaker Hill Road near the corner of Route 44 in the Village of Pleasant Valley, Dutchess County, was once part of a 110-acre farm. The property also included a three-story mill, farmhouse, orchards and a large Dutch barn.

The rear of the fieldstone structure overlooks the Wappinger Creek, which was the source of power for the mill that once existed on the south side of Route 44, then named Filkintown Road.

Known as the Potash House, the structure got its name from early settlers who used potash there to make soap and glass. Potash was also stored there for the Continental Army during the American Revolution.

Potash is any of various mined and manufactured salts that contain potassium in water-soluble form. The name derives from pot ash, which refers to plant ashes soaked in water in a pot, the primary means of manufacturing the product before the industrial era.

During the American Revolution, potash was used by the Continental Army to make gunpowder. After the war, the building served various purposes. During the 1860s it was used as the community's general store and post office. It then became a single-family residence for many years. During the 1940s it was converted into a fashionable tea room.

Ernest I. Hatfield, a New York state senator representing the 34th and 35th districts from 1948 through 1964, acquired the building in the mid-1950s and based his thriving real estate and insurance business in it. Poughkeepsie's Jim Smith is the grandson of Hatfield and, along with the Potash House, he inherited and operates two of three area farms that the state senator once owned.

The Hatfield's of Westchester County were a very well-known family and the Battle of White Plains was actually fought on a hill at the Gilbert Hatfield farm, which was owned by Smith's great-grandfather. His grandfather eventually set down roots in Poughkeepsie around 1910 and became an alderman there.

Hatfield originally operated his real estate business at 46 Cannon Street in Poughkeepsie but he sought to move it outside of the city boundaries and discovered the Potash House. Attracted to its history, Hatfield purchased the building after the tea house closed.

He'd always had an intense interest in historic structures and, on two occasions during the 1950s, Hatfield was instrumental is saving one of Poughkeepsie's most treasured sites, the Clinton House on Main Street.

When the state announced plans to demolish the Clinton House, Hatfield saved it for the Daughters of the American Revolution, who were then housed in the building. He fought hard to rescue the building by appealing to the state legislature.

In 2001, Poughkeepsie attorney Fred Schaeffer rented Potash House to use as a branch office for his Poughkeepsie practice. Schaeffer is also Pleasant Valley's town historian.

At one time, between a covered bridge that once spanned the Wappinger Creek (now replaced by a concrete overpass) along Rt. 44 and the Potash House, there was a harness maker's shop. Through the years, artifacts related to that operation have been uncovered at the site.

The Potash House is located at 31 Quaker Hill Road, Pleasant Valley.

Poughkeepsie Regatta

The Cornell boathouse is the last remaining original structure from the Poughkeepsie Regatta era.

An annual Intercollegiate Rowing Association (IRA) Championship was held on the Hudson River at Poughkeepsie, Dutchess County, from 1895 to 1949 except during the two world wars. The annual competition attracted tens of thousands of spectators to cheer on their favorite college crew.

Founded by Cornell University, the University of Pennsylvania, and Columbia University, the IRA selected the Hudson River location near Marist College in Poughkeepsie primarily for its four-mile straightaway in that vicinity.

Poughkeepsie was a thriving city at the time. It had train service from Grand Central Terminal as well as the day liner from New York City, so spectators had several ways to attend the competition.

Over time as other colleges joined the competition, a number of boathouses were built alongside the east bank of the river to house both boats and crew members. The crews typically arrived in Poughkeepsie a week or so before the competition to practice. That area was dubbed Regatta Row.

The event became so closely identified with its host community that it was soon referred to as the Poughkeepsie Regatta. The day's festivities included a parade, music and street vendors selling college banners and pins.

Spectators could gather in boats along the banks of the river or sit in an observation train on the West Shore Railroad tracks, which traveled along the race route as the teams moved on the river. Spectators sat in bleachers that had been erected on flatbed rail cars.

The regatta became the premier college rowing event in the country. It held the same stature in college athletics that the Rose Bowl and the Army-Navy football game do today.

Depending on the number of crews and schools entered in the competition, a two-mile freshman and three-mile junior varsity race were held in addition to the four-mile varsity race. Cornell won the first varsity championship in 1895.

In 1923, the University of Washington became the first college from the west to participate in the competition. Over the years, their crew won several championships. Navy and the University of California also sent crews to compete.

In 1949, the regatta relocated from Poughkeepsie to a new home on a lake in Marietta, Ohio. One year later, local high schools including Poughkeepsie, Arlington and Roosevelt began to use the abandoned boathouses and compete on the Hudson River.

The regatta relocated again in 1952 to Syracuse, New York, and then to Camden, New Jersey, in 1995.

Of the original boathouses located along Regatta Row in Poughkeepsie, only one remains. In more recent times, Marist meticulously restored the Cornell boathouse and it now serves as a multi-purpose facility. The college also built a newer boathouse just south of the Cornell structure, which is used by its men's and women's crew teams. It stands on the grounds once occupied by the University of California and University of Washington boathouses.

In October 2008, the Hudson River Rowing Association staged a revival of the regatta with races in eight classifications on a 2.3-mile portion of the original route in Poughkeepsie. The following year, as part of the celebration of the 400th anniversary of Henry Hudson's exploration of the Hudson River, Marist College hosted a reenactment of the Poughkeepsie Regatta at Longview Park, the original site of regatta row.

Participating in the 2009 event were rowing crews from Marist, Columbia, Navy, University of Pennsylvania, Cornell, Syracuse, Army and Vassar College.

Regatta Row can be accessed at the western boundary of Marist College and can also be observed from the Walkway over the Hudson, just south of the campus. Today, Marist College rowing crews navigate the same stretch of river as the legendary Poughkeepsie Regatta for all their home competitions.

Quitman House

The historic wood-frame house that sits on the west side of Route 9, approximately 2½ miles north of Rhinebeck, Dutchess County, was built in 1798 as a parsonage for the pastor of St. Peter the Apostle Church. The land it occupies was purchased in 1729 from Robert Gilbert Livingston.

A wood-frame church was constructed there by a group of Lutherans in what was then the original Rhinebeck settlement. In 1783, the stone church that stands on the site today was built right over the wooden church. When work began on the stone church's interior, the wooden structure was taken down.

As the congregation grew, a decision was made to call a pastor and build a parsonage for him in 1797.

The Rev. Friedrich Quitman, a preacher who was in high standing in the hierarchy of the American Lutheran church, was hired as the congregation's first pastor. He came to Rhinebeck after serving as pastor of a Lutheran congregation in Curacao, the West Indies, for the previous twelve years.

The parsonage was comprised of ten rooms. Quitman kept his large bed in a space that would later be used as a dining room. Weighing in excess of 330 pounds, Quitman had a large iron ring installed over his bed affixed with a heavy rope, with which he could pull himself upright and out of bed each morning.

He routinely preached at the church while seated in a large armchair on the altar.

During Quitman's tenure at St. Peter – also known as the Old Stone Church or the Old German Church – its records were kept in English, with many of the old German names anglicized. Few people spoke German any longer.

Throughout his years as pastor, Quitman baptized more than 1,500 children and performed 708 marriages. As the church continued to grow, Quitman oversaw a complete renovation of the original church. He hired Stephen McCarty to handle the project at a cost of $3,000.

Quitman and his wife had seven children, three of which went on to achieve distinguished careers in their own right. William became a local physician and his brother Henry became the Town of Rhinebeck's supervisor during the 1830s.

John Anthony Quitman, whose name is prominently displayed on a state-erected historic marker in front of the house during the 1930s, was a lawyer and soldier. He was a judge, a member of the Mississippi state legislature and subsequently a congressman and governor of that state.

Among other lasting tributes bestowed in his honor, the town of Quitman, Mississippi, and Fort Quitman on the Rio Grande River in Texas are named for him. The fort was named for him due to his meritorious service as a major general in the Mexican-American War.

Failing health forced Dr. Quitman to retire in 1828 after being pastor in Rhinebeck for three decades. Following Quitman's death in 1832, there was a decline in the congregation's membership at St. Peter due, in part, to the growth of surrounding villages and the establishment of Lutheran churches in those communities.

In 1860, St. Peter's broke with the Lutheran Synod, a church body that consists of many churches practicing the same beliefs and ideals. The departure of the Rhinebeck congregation from the Synod resulted in more congregants leaving the church. It also made finding a new pastor a difficult task.

Despite that fact, renovations on the church were undertaken and, in 1870, a new pulpit, platform and furniture were put in place. In 1882, a pipe organ was installed and, eight years later, a set of stain glass windows were added. Those windows were eventually removed.

During that era, John Blackhouse Astor Jr. began to amass a huge amount of property In Rhinebeck, buying several houses and demolishing them. Many of them belonged to the remaining congregants at St. Peter, which caused yet another decline in membership at the church.

The land holding would pass on to his son, John Jacob Astor, who established the Ferncliff estate overlooking the Hudson River. Astor was also among the victims who perished in the sinking of the Titanic in April 1912.

St. Peter's continued to function as a weekly house of worship until 1939, when its members finally went back to a quarterly meeting status, the minimum activity that was necessary to qualify as a separate church entity. The area's Lutheran churches still hold occasional services there, and a small local church group meets there.

The parsonage continued to be occupied by St. Peter's pastors until 1929, when the house became a rental property. During the 1970s, it faced demolition. However, a group of concerned citizens got permission to restore the then-deteriorating structure and bring it back to its original state. In 1976, the Quitman Resource Center for Preservation was founded to meet that objective.

Today, as the Museum of Rhinebeck History, the Quitman house hosts various events and functions and volunteers welcome visitors. It is open to the public from 1-4 p.m. on Saturdays from May through late September. It is located at 7015 Route 9, Rhinebeck.

Rest Haven

Situated on a slight hill on the west side of High Street in the Village of Monroe, Orange County, is the opulent two-story Colonial Revival-style wood mansion built in 1903 for wealthy hop broker and grain exporter Charles McKendrick and his family. A native of Canada, McKendrick maintained an office in Manhattan by the 1890s. He had learned the business from his father Quinton.

McKendrick purchased the Monroe property in 1901 for $692.50. It included three separate parcels that, combined, totaled nearly eleven acres. The home was designed by architect Arthur C. Longyear and built by the Welch brothers, Warwick-based contractors.

Longyear originally had offices in New York City but as his workload increased in the Hudson Valley, he relocated and operated out of Kingston, Ulster County.

Constructed on a large scale with lavish finishes and both colonial and neoclassical architectural features, the stately residence was meant to reflect the stature and wealth of the McKendrick family. Its nearly rectangular shape is distinctive in that it boasts two large and one small hipped-roof blocks. The two large ones feature intersecting gable roofs and roof dormers.

The home's interior features a high level of sophisticated workmanship. The flooring on the first floor is laid in parquet with contrasting oak and mahogany in various patterns. The woodwork, sweeping staircases, fireplaces and Ionic columns throughout the dwelling are of the highest quality material and craftsmanship.

For two decades after the mansion was built, it served as an elegant country estate for the McKendrick family, often making headlines in local newspapers whenever a significant function took place there. But the structure would soon become better known for its next use, starting in the mid-1920s.

In 1923, Moses C. Migel, another Monroe resident who achieved his own considerable fortune in the silk manufacturing industry, purchased the mansion. Having placed his thriving business in the hands of others, Migel focused on his philanthropy and the former family residence would become the center of one of his most passionate projects.

Two years before acquiring the house, Migel assisted in the establishment of the American Foundation for the Blind and served as its first president. In that role he provided significant financial support and served as an officer. When he became aware of the "war of the dots" – a longstanding feud between proponents of the New York Point (letters printed with movable type from which stereotype plates were cast) and the sponsors of American braille (a popular braille alphabet used in the United States before the adoption of standardized English braille) – he was appointed head of the commission on Uniform Type for the Blind.

Migel's plan for the former McKendrick mansion was to convert it into a summer retreat – named Rest Haven – for blind girls and women in New York City. During two-week stays, the blind visitors enjoyed a relaxing vacation in Monroe, all expenses paid including rail transportation to and from the site.

In a September 1923 article featured in the Brooklyn Standard Union newspaper, interested parties were advised to contact Miss M.J. Johnson to make arrangements for a stay at the facility.

In part, the article read "It is a private enterprise started by a wealthy man who has been interested in work for the blind for the last 20 years. As he wants to keep his identity a secret, all arrangements are made with Miss Johnson. Applicants register with her and when a sufficiently large group is assembled she arranges for some sighted companions to go with them."

Rest Haven regularly accepted twenty blind female visitors at a time, along with five sighted attendants for the two-week stints.

Migel's involvement with a number of initiatives for the blind gained him the friendship of deaf-blind American author, political activist and lecturer Helen Keller. In October 1931, Keller and her teacher Anne Sullivan spent time at Migel's 230-acre country estate named Greenbraes Farm. Keller visited Rest Haven on many occasions. There are several photographs of her taken during a visit in 1950.

By the 1940s, blind guests were arriving from as far away as Glens Falls in the Adirondacks as well as from Cattaraugus County in southwestern New York.

Migel died in 1958 at the age of ninety, but Rest Haven continued to operate through 1967 when the American Foundation for the Blind decided to close the facility. By then, there were other camps for the blind in New York and New England, and the foundation had other projects to support.

The stately structure is now owned by HRR Corporation and sits at 236 High St., Monroe.

Skinny House

There are a number of narrow or "skinny" houses that were built for a variety of reasons throughout the world. Some of them are also known as "spite" houses because they were built primarily to bring distress to a neighbor. One such home said to be the oldest in the United States is located in Marblehead, Massachusetts, and was erected in 1716.

Legend has it that two brothers were involved in a disagreement over a parcel of land. Despite the ongoing argument, one of the siblings built a stately wood-frame house on land that had a beautiful view of Salem Sound. In response, his angered brother built a ten-foot wide home in front of the other, all but blocking his brother's spectacular view.

By contrast, a "skinny" home that was built in 1932 and stands on Grand Street in Mamaroneck, Westchester County, was the result of one neighbor's kindness to another.

Nathan Seely was a self-educated African American carpenter who, with his brother Willard, established the Seely Brothers Construction Company around the time when the movement called the Great Migration began. Starting in 1916, a large number of black folks left the southern states in favor of living in the north.

The Seely brothers built quality but affordable homes catering to the black southerners arriving in lower Westchester. The Seelys purchased a number of parcels of land in Mamaroneck and built homes for the new residents. The opening paragraph in the company's printed brochure – titled Homes for Colored People – started with "Every colored man needs a home."

As the business grew, Nathan and Willard Seely hired a secretary and a lawyer and bought a fleet of six Mack trucks. In 1926, Nathan Seely designed and built a seven-room house for his family at 173 Grand St., one that featured many of the most modern amenities of the day.

Unfortunately, when the stock market crashed in 1929, kicking off the Great Depression, it had a profound effect on the Seely enterprise. The financial downturn not only forced the Seely business into bankruptcy but also caused Seely to lose his Grand Street residence.

In 1931, an Italian immigrant named Panfilo Santangelo, who lived next door to Seely's former house (on land that Seely had sold him), decided to earmark a 12½ by100-foot strip of his property for Seely to build a new house for his family. The strip of land sat between Santangelo's house and the house that Seely had lost to foreclosure.

The following year, lacking the funds for materials, Seely relied upon his ability to salvage and recycle items, including windows, banisters and even a chicken coop, which became part of the living room. A center beam Seely installed in the full basement had been a rusted railroad track from a defunct line.

The resulting red shingled, multi-gable roofed "skinny house" spans ten feet wide and thirty-seven feet long. It has three floors and its interior walls are made of paperboard hammered into wood scraps. Out of consideration for his wife Lillian, Seely added a ledge for flowerpots outside, under a second story window.

Seely fastened the house to the ground using steel cables on each side that are still visible today. They ensure that a heavy wind will not blow the house over.

Nathan Seely passed away in 1962. Members of his family continued to live in the house through 1986. A neighbor and the daughter of Panfilo Santangelo purchased the house in 1988 for $30,000 from Seely's daughter, who was then in a nursing home. In effect, the transaction returned the land's ownership back to the Santangelos. Since then, the house has been used as rental property.

The original house that Panfilo Santangelo occupied is now in the hands of his granddaughter, who, with her mother, has maintained the "skinny house" through the years. Mother and daughter considered a complete renovation of the tiny house in recent years, but the discovery of a serious termite infestation put an end to their plans.

The "skinny house" was added to the National Register of Historic Places in 2015, and the mother-daughter team is now considering turning the structure over to the local historical society. With the registry status, the society would be able to obtain grants to fix the damage caused by termites.

The "skinny house" is located at 175 Grand St., Mamaroneck.

While in the town, you might want to visit another unique building, also on the National Register of Historic Places. Walter's Hot Dog Stand on Palmer Avenue was built in 1928 in Mamaroneck and to date remains a popular eatery in town. It belonged to Walter Harrington.

A striking presence in the village, the rectangular, one-story building attracts attention from passersby due to its steeply pitched hip roof that features cooper tiles and elaborate Chinese ornamentation.

Hot dogs became popular during the late 19th century. They were served at Coney Island beach in Brooklyn and at professional baseball games.

Harrington already owned an apple orchard and cider press, and he eventually added hot dogs to his offerings at a roadside stand. But they weren't just any hot dogs. Harrington had an agreement with a meat maker, and the two men developed a unique recipe, one that is still well guarded and used today.

He also started to split and grill the hot dogs, which is a trademark process still in use at the stand.

As for the building's architecture, Harrington relied on the work of a Chinese friend who lived in Connecticut to draw up the plans. His only requirement was that the structure had to be attractive, unusual and strong; the plans undoubtedly met those requirements.

Still family-run at 937 Palmer Ave., across the street from Mamaroneck High School, Walter's Hot Dog Stand is a terrific place to stop for lunch or a snack while searching out hidden treasures in the area.

Smith Tavern Complex

On Bedford Avenue (Route 22) in the Town of Armonk, Westchester County, sits Smith Tavern, a two-story wood frame building that dates to the late 18th century. During its early days, the tavern provided ideal accommodations for travelers along Danbury Post Road and became a social and political meeting place to debate local issues.

The original proprietor was Benjamin Hopkins, a Quaker who was known to have taken in people who escaped New York City during the American Revolution. At the time, the city was a stronghold for British troops. As the war intensified, Hopkins fled north to Fishkill, Dutchess County, hoping to settle in a more neutral community.

Hopkins rented his tavern to Ichabod Ogden before he left. In 1779, the structure sustained serious damage when British troops set it ablaze, along with other houses in the area. A contingent of the Continental Army's militia forces is said to have occupied the house as its headquarters at the time of the fire.

When the war finally ended, political gatherings to organize towns in the region took place at the tavern. Its then owner, Benjamin Tripp, eventually sold the tavern to Harrison Palmer, who was elected the town clerk in 1791. That transaction ensured that future meetings would continue to be held there.

Captain John Smith, who served with the Continental Army and was captured during the Revolutionary War, became the establishment's next owner, as well as the newly elected town clerk in 1798. A tailor by trade, it is said that British officers spared him severe punishment while he was in captivity in exchange for his making fine clothing for them.

Because of Smith's local stature and position in politics, the tavern became the site of a variety of political functions, elections, rallies and debates. When the North Castle Post Office was established in 1809 and located in a portion of the tavern, as was commonplace at that time, Smith was named the town's first postmaster. He also oversaw a general store that stood adjacent to the tavern but is now long gone.

As stagecoach travel started to flourish, it became a regular overnight stop for the stage line. Smith's son Samuel soon joined his father in operating the various aspects of the business and following the elder Smith's death, he continued to run it. Following in his dad's footsteps, Samuel Smith was elected town clerk in 1830, holding the position for the next twenty-five years.

By the mid-19th century with the arrival of the railroad, the use of stagecoaches in the region dwindled quickly. That fact and the development of other communities around New Castle caused Smith Tavern's business and status as a meeting place to decline. Samuel Smith died in 1884, and the property was acquired by Odle Knapp, who was a successful farmer from Greenwich, Connecticut.

Knapp transferred ownership of the property to his son and daughter-in-law, Augustus and Kate who, in 1898, oversaw extensive renovations to the building, adding a second floor and building a northeast wing. Augustus Knapp ran the farm until his death in 1905, and it was then sold to George Smith (no relation to Captain John Smith).

George Smith's tenure was brief. He sold the tavern and farm separately in 1916. The farm was sold to Charles Mills, and the tavern and seventeen acres was sold to Fay Stanton of New York City. While rooms were still rented in the west wing addition, the tavern had otherwise ceased to operate during the Knapp ownership.

Stanton attempted to reintroduce the tavern operation under a new name, The Red Jacket Inn, but it failed miserably. After only two years, it was sold at a public auction to Manhattan attorney and millionaire John Sterling. Unfortunately, Sterling's death later that year saw the tavern, along with the majority of his vast estate, bequeathed to Yale University.

The college quickly disposed of the aging structure and the old tavern went through two owners who used it as a private residence. In 1974, it fell into the hands of the Christian and Missionary Alliance, which used it as a parsonage and religious education facility. In 1977, the North Castle Historical Society purchased the building and converted it into a museum.

Now known as the Smith's Tavern Educational Complex, the grounds include the tavern/museum, a 1798 Quaker Meeting House, a one-room schoolhouse and the vintage Brundidge Blacksmith Shop.

Visitors can see the oldest part of the tavern where the militia met and town meetings were held, along with the small innkeeper's bedroom just off the kitchen. Captain Smith's original tavern license and a silver caudle cup that is said to have been used by General George Washington are on display, along with many artifacts including household and farm tools.

The 19th-century blacksmith shop, which was originally located diagonally across the road, still features its original forge, anvil and bellows. A one-horse open sleigh with bells is also exhibited at the site. Visit the old schoolhouse to sit in an early "double desk" or at the teacher's desk, which rests on a raised platform.

The Friends Meeting House was relocated from Cox Avenue where, for nearly a century, it was the house of worship for Quakers in North Castle. There, visitors can enter the separate doors for men and women and observe the original wood "separating" partition that was raised and lowered as needed for business meetings.

The Smith's Tavern Educational Complex is run by the historical society and is open for public visits on Wednesdays and Sundays, from 2-4 p.m. It is located at 440 Bedford Road (Route 22), Armonk, New York. For information, call 914-273-4510.

Standard House

Built in 1855, the Standard House in the City of Peekskill, Dutchess County, is a square, three-story, four-by-three bay Italianate style brick commercial building with apartments on its upper floors. It was built during the city's early industrial period as a boarding house and tavern to accommodate businessmen traveling to Peekskill on business – primarily the manufacture of stoves.

Located near to both the New York Central Railroad station and to the adjacent Hudson River, the lodging provided easy access to the extremely active municipality. Initially, the first floor of the building served as a dock store with guest rooms above. In its heyday, it was surrounded by other commercial, industrial and residential buildings.

In 1890, the building was sold to John Galligan, who converted the dock store into a thriving tavern and alehouse. Some years later, Galligan became an enthusiastic supporter of U.S. presidential candidate William Jennings Bryan and, during the 1908 campaign, Bryan spoke to a crowd of two thousand people gathered at the railroad station from the porch of the train's rear parlor car. The following day, a newspaper account of the campaign stop featured a photograph that showed the Standard House prominently featured in the background. Two days later, Bryan's opponent, William Howard Taft, would stop at the same location to campaign to another large gathering.

During Prohibition, from 1920 to 1933, Galligan closed the business and sold the building to John Carbone. Despite the ban on alcohol, Carbone opened a fine dining restaurant, which did very well in the riverside community. When the prohibition era came to an end, he restored liquor service and the business continued to flourish.

When the Carbone family decided to sell the business during the late 1980s, its new owner christened the restaurant the Central Grill. Sadly, when it was damaged significantly by a fire, the building was boarded up. The city began foreclose on the building due to unpaid taxes.

Deteriorating and in need of considerable work, the Standard House got a second lease on life when, in 1998, longtime Peekskill residents Kathy and Rick Cerreta purchased the building with the intention of saving the historical structure. A complete restoration was done to retain its historic features rather than modernize it. In 2000, the building was added to the National Register of Historic Places. It reopened in March 2001.

That same year, Standard House was temporarily transformed to look like a police station during the filming of 20th Century Fox's 2000 release Unfaithful starring Richard Gere and Diane Laine. Unfortunately, scenes filmed at the building were later edited out of the movie.

Standard House, which is located at 50 Hudson Ave. in Peekskill, remains a stunning example of mid-19th century architecture as well as an important part of the once thriving industrial center of Peekskill.

Stissing House

Like many taverns and inns established during the 18th and 19th centuries, Stissing House, located on the southwest corner of South Main (Route 82) and West Church (Route 199) streets in Pine Plains, Dutchess County, operated under numerous owners and various names since it opened in 1782. An iconic structure in town, the building also served as the community's first library and, at one time, housed a physician's office.

Cornelius Elmendorph opened the tavern, originally conducting business from a log house that he built on the site. It was an ideal location for travelers to stop along the Salisbury Turnpike, which ran from the Hudson River to northwest Connecticut. Originally known as Elmendorph's House, its name was changed as new owners acquired it. Through the years, the structure increased in size through a series of expansions.

Ebenezer Baldwin acquired the tavern from Elmendorph in 1797, the same year a meeting was held in the building to form the Union Library of Pine Plains. Baldwin was one of three people who traveled to New York City to purchase the library's first books, which were then housed in the tavern. Baldwin became the town's first librarian.

A number of different owners followed until Henry Myers acquired the building in 1835 and operated it as Myers Motel for the next thirty-two years. The business became a favorite meeting place for local farmers and cattle and sheep drovers guiding their herds southbound from New England to New York City.

In 1882, Albert Bowman purchased the building and immediately christened it Stissing House in honor of a local Indian chief. He also added a porch to the north side of the building.

Prior to 1895, while innkeepers owned the business, the land the building occupied remained part of the estate of George Clarke, one of the original Little Nine Partners Patent. That year, the Clarke property was sold as part of a mortgage foreclosure and the inn and twenty-one acres was purchased by two investors from Germantown.

During the 1890s, a portion of the building's first floor was used as a physician's office. One in a line of physicians to use the space was H. C. Wilber, in whose memory the town's distinctive clock tower was built just south of the inn.

The elegant Stissing House features a beautiful domed ballroom and an extremely rare form of original Dutch Colonial framing. It was the site of numerous society balls, town meetings and political rallies during its heyday. Politicians ranging from George Washington to Franklin D. Roosevelt used Stissing House for campaigning purposes. French General Marquis de Lafayette is among the many prominent guests to have spent a night at the inn.

During the early 20th century, Stissing House became a popular destination for vacationers from New York City as well as a favorite dining spot noted for its home-cooked meals. Over time, the property was divided and sold. The inn retained nearly one acre.

In 1991, Christian Eisenbeiss and Dale Mitchell purchased the building, which had deteriorated significantly through the years. Their primary objective was to restore the historic structure. The foundation walls were raised to stabilize it, a new roof was put on, and about 150 broken panes of glass were replaced.

Today, dinner is still served at the historic Stissing House from Thursday through Sunday. Sunday brunch is also served beginning at noon. Cocktails are served starting at 5 p.m., Thursdays through Saturdays.

Stissing House is located at 7801 South Main St., Pine Plains. For more information, call 518-398-8800.

Stone House Intersection

The four corners at the intersection of Crown and John streets in the Stockade District of the City of Kingston, Ulster County, have the distinction of being the only intersection in the United States to feature four 18th-century stone structures. The four buildings were constructed before the American Revolution and they sustained serious damage in 1777 when British troops stormed the city, which was then the capital of New York State. The British burned virtually every building in the district.

The attack occurred after the British had gained victories downriver at Fort Montgomery and Fort Clinton (near today's Bear Mountain Bridge). They bypassed a chain that had been strung across the Hudson River near Constitution Island and West Point and made their way upriver with plans to participate at the Battle of Saratoga.

The two battles in the Bear Mountain region and their stop to burn Kingston might have cost the British a victory in Saratoga. Their troops didn't make it in time for the battle, resulting in an important Continental Army victory.

Continental Army General George Clinton was sworn in as New York's first governor on the steps of the original Ulster County Courthouse, located in the Stockade District. Clinton relocated the government operation to nearby Hurley until the attack ended. When he and other officials returned, they found the courthouse, churches and residences in the district smoldering from the British-set fires. The community was slowly rebuilt.

Three of the four stone houses at the corner of Crown and John streets were quickly rebuilt by the respective families who lived in them. The fourth, which stood on the northwest corner, was totally destroyed. It was replaced on the same site with a new structure, also made of stone.

The Frantz Roggen house stands on the northeast corner of the intersection, at 42 Crown St. The 1½-story, coursed limestone exterior features its five original bays' layout with a center doorway topped with a Kingston Gable. It featured nine rooms and five fireplaces. A clapboard and shingled extension was added on its north side during the late 19th century.

Following the severe fire damage to the Roggen house, the lot it stood on was used for gallows, used to hang spies during the remainder of the Revolutionary War. That section of the family's property had become designated as public land and, when Roggen decided to repair his house, the family had to pay seven pounds and ten shillings to reclaim it despite the fact that it had originally belonged to them.

Some of the beams inside the house were actually taken from the hangman's scaffold. There is also evidence in the basement of the house that indicates use as a tunnel, with which the family could escape if and when the settlement came under Indian attacks, which is how the Stockade District got its name in the first place.

The district originated in 1658 when Colonial Governor Peter Stuyvesant ordered settlers who had been working farms along the Esopus Creek to move to higher ground. This was deemed necessary due to growing tensions over land disputes that existed between the settlers and the Esopus Indians.

Both settlers and Indians farmed adjacent tracts of land for five years with growing animosity that was reaching a boiling point. About sixty-five European settlers occupied the lowlands when the order came to move to a thirty-two-acre bluff that overlooked their previous community. The settlers painstakingly dismantled their homes and barns, board by board, and reassembled each structure at the new location.

For added protection a 1,300-foot long, 14-foot high stockade fence was built around the bluff. Thus, the Stockade District was born.

The Matthew Persen House occupies the southeastern corner of the famed intersection at 74 John St. When New Netherlands was seized by the British in 1664, the Dutch forces disbanded and Sergeant Jan Persen decided to settle in the Kingston district and build this house.

During the burning of Kingston, Persen's residence was almost completely destroyed, and his family rebuilt it after the attack. When Persen died in 1708, he left the house to his son Matthew. For many years, the building was used as a Public House with living quarters for the family in the rear.

In 1820, the 1½-story house was purchased by Dr. John Goodwin, who added a wing on the John Street side to serve as a drug store and grocery store. Around the turn of the 20th century, the house was acquired by Ulster County, and it was converted for use as county offices.

Across the street from the Persen house, at 82 John St., sits a stone building that was constructed in 1774. It opened in May 1777 as the Kingston Academy, which specialized in classical and academic education. It has the distinction of having been the first academy to open in the state. New York State Governor DeWitt Clinton and renowned artist John Vanderlyn are among the school's well-known graduates.

The academy was eventually incorporated into the City of Kingston school system, after which the building was used by a cabinet maker. During the 20th century, The Kingston Daily Leader, a local newspaper, operated from the building.

The last of the four stone houses at the intersection is on the site of the original Matthew Janssen House, at 43 Crown St., which was built in 1700. The two-story structure sustained considerable damage during the British attack and all but one room – which is said to be incorporated into the rebuilt house – was destroyed.

Matthew Janssen reconstructed the house after the American Revolution and, by 1820, it was owned and occupied by John and Katie Jansen. Like many of the structures in the district, this house went through a series of owners and uses through the years.

In 1866, it was purchased by John Hardenburgh, who was an attorney, a delegate to the New York State Constitutional Convention and later a state senator. His law office was located next door. By 1901, dentist J.C. Norton and his family lived in the house; his daughter Clara Norton Reed, a reporter for the local Daily Freeman newspaper, lived in it through 1930.

From 1950 on, the building served as a music studio, advertising service, insurance and security bonds business, and then back to a private residence.

Kingston's Stockade District boasts other places of interest that include the second Ulster County Court House, which replaced the original burned down in 1777. It is where African-American abolitionist Sojourner Truth successfully tried her case to recover her son, who had been illegally transferred out of state to continue a life in slavery. The Senate House, where the state of New York was established is also in the Stockade District. So is the Old Dutch Church where George Washington visited and Governor George Clinton is interred.

But the four corners that make up the intersection of Crown and John streets remains an intriguing locale as the only site in North America to feature stone houses on all four corners, each with a fascinating history of its own.

Stoutenburgh Family Cemetery

L ocated at the north end of Doty Avenue in the Town of Hyde
Park, Dutchess County, the one-acre Stoutenburgh Family Cemetery, which was established in 1768, is the last tract of land owned
by descendants of the first family to settle in the town. Positioned
just south of the Vanderbilt estate and adjacent to a community park
west of Route 9 the cemetery sat close to the long gone Jacobus
Stoutenburgh home.

Born in New York City in 1696, Stoutenburgh was the first person
to settle in today's Hyde Park, a community originally named for
him. He built a Dutch manor house in 1741 at today's intersection
of West Market Street and Park Place. In fact, today's West Market
Street originated as a driveway that Stoutenburgh built to access his
home from King's Highway (later Albany Post Road; today's Route
9). He planted cherry trees on both sides of the drive to enhance the
entrance.

Stoutenburgh was a merchant, farmer, yeoman, and judge who
amassed a considerable amount of property in the region. Shortly
after he settled into his new home with his wife Margaret (Teller)
and their eight children, he and a son-in-law, Major Richard De
Cantillon, built a dock and boat landing on the Hudson River, which
was known as the De Cantillon and Stoutenburgh Landing.

In 1777, while making their way north where they would eventually burn down the City of Kingston, British troops destroyed the landing by firing upon it from passing ships. The Stoutenburgh family home, which sat farther up the road from the river, also came under attack. The family of staunch Patriots fled, taking up temporary residence at son William's home on today's Violet Avenue (Route 9G), just south of East Market Street.

Because of the elevation of the house in relation to the British vessels on the Hudson River, it did not sustain significant damage during the attack. Only one twenty-four-pound cannonball made it through the lower panel of the westerly Dutch door. It grazed the floor and exited through the opposite Dutch door. Another cannonball missed the house completely and landed nearby on the property.

By 1870, Jacobus Stoutenburgh's home was in severe disrepair and was taken down when the municipality decided to extend West Market Street (Stoutenburgh's original driveway) west to what is now known as the Upper Landing. Today, the house would have stood right in the middle of West Market Street. While that house did not survive, Southenburgh's son William's residence and another one owned by his brother John (on the east side of Route 9 across from Mansion Drive in the Village of Hyde Park) are the only remaining Dutch Colonial stone houses in the town.

Until recently, John's residence was occupied by a Japanese restaurant, which relocated to Poughkeepsie in 2012. The building is now the office of a New York State senator.

Local tax records identify about seventy-five farms that, through the years, were established on land that was originally owned by Jacobus Stoutenburgh. Today, the burial ground at the end of Doty Avenue, along with the Willian Stoutenburgh house on Violet Avenue are the only parcels of land that remain in the descendants' possession under their organization, the Stoutenburgh-Teller Family Association.

The association was founded in August 1942, acquired the family burial ground and established an endowment fund for its upkeep. Jacobus Stoutenbergh was the first person buried in the cemetery and his (and his wife's) gravestones are located in the most northwest portion of the grounds. The entrance to the cemetery was originally located on its north side but Frederick Vanderbilt objected to visitors walking through his estate to access it.

Vanderbilt went as far as to attempt to purchase the cemetery but the Stoutenburgh family would not allow it. In 1937, the descendants relocated the entrance to the south side, ensuring that no one visiting the grounds would have to infringe on the Vanderbilt property.

That same year, on June 19, the pillars and gates that grace the cemetery's entrance were a gift from descendent Eugene Cantin in memory of his wife Roberta Louise. They were dedicated in a formal ceremony and one pillar features the history of the cemetery's founding on a bronze plaque. In October 2012, the cemetery – with the permission of the family association – became a geocache site, a real-world outdoor treasure hunting game. Players attempt to locate hidden containers (called geocaches), using GPS-enabled devices and a series of published coordinates, then they share their findings on the Internet.

The town changed its name from Stoutenburgh to Hyde Park around

The gates that grace the cemetery entrance were a gift from descendant Eugene Cantin

1804, when the owner of the Hyde Park Inn, much to the chagrin of Dr. John Bard (who's estate boasted that name), lifted the name without permission for his establishment. He applied to the government for permission to include a post office in the inn. Someone in the government office, not knowing the town's history, granted the request thinking that the name of the tavern was the community's name. The Hyde Park name was officially adopted by the town in 1821.

Jacobus Stoutenburgh is depicted in the third of a nineteen-panel mural in the Hyde Park Post Office lobby, which shows the early settler working the land prior to his home's construction. He is also mentioned on a bronze plaque on the north wall at the front entrance of Hyde Park Town Hall. Another marker was also placed on the southwest corner of West Market Street and Park Place to identify the site of his 1741 home.

To visit the historic cemetery from Route 9, turn west onto West Market Street (across from the Hyde Park Post Office), make a right turn heading north onto Doty Avenue and proceed to the end of the road.

Thomas Paine Cottage

Sitting on the west side of Sicard Avenue in New Rochelle, Westchester County, is the two-story, saltbox house that was home to English-born philosopher, political activist and revolutionary writer Thomas Paine. Although Paine traveled a great deal during his prolific career, he lived in this home from 1802 to 1806.

Among the best example of the power of the pen are the complete works of Paine, who supported both the French and American revolutions with his series of pamphlets such as Common Sense and The Age of Reason, both of which brought unity in support of independence in both countries. It is documented that his The American Crisis pamphlet series provided much-needed inspiration and emotional strength to the Continental Army during their fight for independence in 1776.

Born in Thetford, England, in 1737, Paine's formal education ended at the age of thirteen when his family's poverty forced him into taking an apprenticeship to earn money. He held several jobs between 1757 and 1774 after leaving home at the age of nineteen.

Paine spent his leisure hours attending lectures and reading extensively. During his time in London, Paine met and made a favorable impression on Benjamin Franklin, who would go on to become one of the Founding Fathers of the United States.

In October 1774, Paine decided to travel to the New World and, with Franklin's help, he set out for Philadelphia, arriving just in time to take part in the American Revolution. Once settled in Philadelphia, he began by submitting articles to Pennsylvania Magazine, overseen by publisher Robert Aitkens.

His first mission of choice reflected in his writing was the abolition of Negro slavery. When the two-shilling pamphlet Common Sense was released on Jan. 10, 1776, the forty-seven-page work became an immediate sensation. Approximately 120,000 copies were sold in the first three months, and it is said that virtually every rebel involved in the war for independence read or had it read to them.

While continuing to inspire many with his written word, Paine also enlisted in the Continental Army in time to join the retreat across New Jersey.

In April 1777, Congress appointed Paine secretary of the committee on foreign affairs; two years later he was named clerk of the Pennsylvania Assembly. In 1784, in recognition of both his inspirational writings and direct support of the Continental Army, New York State presented Paine with Loyalist Frederick Davoue's 277-acre farm, which had been confiscated from him during the war. In addition, Pennsylvania legislators awarded Paine £500.

In 1787, Paine left for Europe, dividing his time between England and France. The French Revolution began two years later and Paine became the self-appointed missionary of world revolution. He was imprisoned in Luxembourg Prison in France in 1793 because he was an Englishman, but he was released the following year at the request of the new American minister, James Monroe.

Paine returned to the United States in 1802 at the invitation of President Thomas Jefferson, and he promptly took up residence at his farm in New Rochelle. He maintained other houses in New York City and Bordentown, New Jersey.

The original stone farmhouse formerly occupied by Davoue was destroyed by fire in 1793 during Paine's time in France. When he returned, Paine moved into a cottage on the property. It featured a central chimney and gable roof, its exterior walls covered with shingles.

In 1804, Paine added a one-story frame wing to the structure, spanning eighteen feet wide and twenty-three feet deep with a porch across its front. The first floor of the cottage has a kitchen, a small room heated with a Franklin stove and one bedroom, while the second level boasts four additional bedrooms.

Paine enjoyed his life at the cottage, but he left for New York City in 1806 after being denied the right to vote in New Rochelle. It was in Greenwich Village that Paine died on June 8, 1809. His remains were transported back to New Rochelle because he wished to be buried in a Quaker cemetery. Paine's father had been a Quaker.

Sadly, he was denied that request in his will by the Quakers and his body was buried under a walnut tree on his farm. Only six mourners attended Paine's funeral. Ten years later, the English agrarian journalist William Cobbett dug up Paine's remains and transported them back to England to give Paine a hero's burial, but that never came to be. When Cobbett died twenty years later, his personal effects included Paine's remains but they have since been lost.

When the farm was purchased by Charles See, who subdivided it for real estate development, the Huguenot Association acquired the cottage and relocated it approximately 440 yards west to its current location. In 2009, the cottage went through an extensive renovation to look like it did during Paine's occupancy.

Today, along with the Sophia Brewster one-room schoolhouse (the oldest private school in New Rochelle, which has been moved to the Paine property), the Thomas Paine Cottage and Museum welcomes visitors Thursdays through Sundays, from 10 a.m.-5 p.m. The suggested donation is $5 for adults and $3 for children under 12. It is located at 20 Sicard Ave., New Rochelle. For more information, call 914-633-1776.

Vassar Brothers Institute

The Victorian-Italianate-Gothic style three-story, three-bay building on the west side of today's Vassar Street in the City of Poughkeepsie was built in 1882 on the site of James Vassar's (father of Matthew) former brewery. The brewery was destroyed in a massive fire in 1811. Financed by Matthew Vassar Jr. and John Guy Vassar, nephews of Matthew Vassar, who in 1865 had founded his namesake college in the town, it cost $30,000 to build and is one of a number of the siblings' philanthropic initiatives.

The Vassar brothers recognized the need for a base of operations for two educational societies established in the city during the 1870s: the Poughkeepsie Literacy Club and the Poughkeepsie Society of Natural Sciences. The literacy club, founded in 1869, saw its programs grow in popularity, so much so that the club kept moving its meetings to larger quarters prior to the Institute's construction, including the hall at the YMCA, at the Congregational Church and, finally, at the Lafayette Street Baptist Church.

The Institute building was designed by architect John A. Wood, who designed several other buildings in Poughkeepsie, including the 1869 Collingwood Opera House (now the Bardavon), the gates and gatehouse of the Poughkeepsie Rural Cemetery and the Poughkeepsie Alms House, among others.

An interesting fact about the Vassar Institute design is that, following its completion, Wood was hired to build the Akin Free Library atop Quaker Hill in Pawling. He used the same design as the Vassar Institute. The major difference in the appearance between the two structures is that Wood used red brick with white mortar in Poughkeepsie and granite stone on the Quaker Hill building.

Both buildings include a heavy square portico at their front entrance and feature a tower above their respective mansard roofs, which were designed in an Italianate style.

The two educational societies eventually merged to form the Vassar Brothers Institute, and the Poughkeepsie building was presented to the trustees of the joint organization on Nov. 28, 1882. The structure contained a museum, a science and natural history library, arts studio and a first-floor auditorium that seated more than two hundred people. On its third floor was a studio for sculpture and drawing enthusiasts.

The last president of the literacy club, Vassar College Professor Truman J. Backus, was named as the first president of the institute. Three sections of the Vassar Institute sponsored lectures presented primarily by Vassar College professors. As time passed, well-known personalities from different fields were invited to present talks in the building. The Institute offered weekly lectures every Tuesday during winter.

One of the series' most renowned speakers was Hiram Bingham, a Yale University professor who is credited with the 1911 discovery of the largely forgotten Incan city of Machu Picchu in Peru. Following the discovery, Bingham embarked on an extensive speaking tour with one stop in Poughkeepsie.

In addition to the programs, classes and musical performances held regularly at the Vassar Brothers Institute, farmers and fruit growers in the region also benefited by the Institute's collection of local insects, birds, minerals and other natural science artifacts. Some of its rooms were also used by the Eastman Business College.

The Tuesday Club, founded in 1899 and consisting of about fifty women, many of whom were Vassar College graduates, used the building for weekly meetings. The group's Choral Club performed a private concert in the auditorium every spring. During the 1930s, a community theater group staged various plays in the building.

By 1946, the membership and attendance at the lecture series had increased considerably and the Institute outgrew the original building. The group relocated its popular program to the Poughkeepsie High School auditorium, where it continued for many years. In 1983, the Institute introduced the Science in your Life lecture series. The programs are still held in Poughkeepsie's Our Lady of Lourdes High School auditorium.

During the late 1960s, the Vassar Brothers Institute building was rarely used and had deteriorated to a state of disrepair. The structure was sold in 1977 along with the Vassar Home for Aged Men – another philanthropic endeavor initiated by the Vassar siblings, located down the street from the Vassar Brothers Institute building. The two buildings became the Cunneen-Hackett Arts Center.

The former Vassar Home for Aged Men at 9 Vassar Street, Poughkeepie.

The three-story mens' home was built in 1880 on the site of Matthew Vassar's home. Also designed by Wood, it was established to house fifty men who met the criteria of being at least sixty-five years old, Protestant, and residents of New York State.

Following Cunneen-Hackett's acquisition, the first floor of the former mens' home was transformed into galleries and used for public

209

and private events, while the upper floors serve as office space for other local non-profit organizations.

The Vassar Brothers Institute auditorium was renovated and some of the remaining space was turned into a 1,200-square-foot dance studio, artists' lofts, a music instruction studio, and art galleries. The former Vassar Home for Aged Men is at 9 Vassar St. while the former Vassar Brothers Institute is at 12 Vassar St.

For more information about programs and events at both sites, call 845-486-4571 or visit online at www.cunneen-hackett.org.

Village of Bedford

This former country store and post office is now headquarters for the Bedford Historical Society.

The name Bedford, both town and village first appeared in town records in 1683. Its original name was Hoppground, which is due to the many wild hop vines growing in the settlement. The community is located in Westchester County.

Adhering to New England tradition, the original settlers reserved a three-acre parcel of land to serve as a village common. This section was earmarked to include a meeting house, a burial ground and a grist mill that sat adjacent to the Mianus River.

House lots were laid out and each owner was given three acres of land. A train band – or militia – was organized and a man was selected to beat a drum to gather people in the village for a church service, town meeting or to sound an alarm.

The first houses built are on today's Pound Ridge Road. While some food was acquired from Native Americans in the area, most settlers provided for themselves, importing very little to survive. Wild animals near the village was in plentiful supply, including bear, deer, wild turkey, ducks, geese, and fish from the brooks and rivers.

During the Revolutionary War, Bedford sat between the American and British lines. It was considered neutral ground, but it still experienced raids by British soldiers, who stole cattle for food. The British also destroyed some of the houses.

By July 1779, all but one house had been burned down by the British. It took some time to rebuild the houses, and it took until 1783 to reconstruct the village's landmark Presbyterian Church. Still, today's village boasts a quaint and charming New England appearance, which was its original founders' intention.

Today, Bedford Village features ten historic buildings around the village green. The Bedford Historical Society, which was founded in 1916, is credited with maintaining the buildings and for operating two museums. One is located inside the 1787 Courthouse and the other inside the 1829 stone one-room schoolhouse.

Built the same year that the United States Constitution was adopted, the court house at 615 Old Post Road is the oldest Westchester County government building and one of only three courthouses in New York State built before 1800. Restored in 1889 and again during the late 1960s, it features the Bedford Museum on its second level.

The museum was originally located in the 1829 schoolhouse, which ceased to function as a school in 1912. From 1913 to 1969, it housed the museum collection, which is now in the courthouse. Starting in 2004, the schoolhouse – often called the Stone Jug – went through an extensive renovation to reflect its original purpose.

Built in 1829, this stone one-room schoolhouse is often called the "Stone Jug."

While the desks on display in the structure today date to the early 20th century, the historical society hopes to locate and install wooden desks from 1829, when the educational facility first opened. Tours of the two museums are by appointment or – during summer months – offered on weekends.

Another interesting building in the village is the public library, which was once the Bedford Academy, one of Westchester's first classical schools. Opened on June 6, 1809, the academy operated through 1902, at which time Miss Eloise Laquer organized a library in one of the former school's rooms.

The Corporation of Bedford Academy donated the building to the historical society in 1972 and the Bedford Free Library continues to lease it from the society for $1 per year. The society continues to preserve the building, which is located at 32 Village Green.

Just down the street at 40 Village Green is a Federal to Greek Revival-style structure, built in 1838 as the harness shop of Benjamin Ambler. Since 1893, it has been used as the village's post office. The building was purchased by the historical society in 1972.

On the corner of Guard Hill and Succabone roads stands a distinctive brick tower with an interesting background. Named the Sutton Clock Tower and built in the late 1880s by the Sutton family, who moved from New York City to Bedford. Mrs. Sutton was homesick and distressed over not being able to hear the city's church bells.

In response, James Sutton, her husband and a successful New York art dealer, had a huge clock erected in their barn's cupola. It was a time and strike model with a 550-pound bell. All was well until, in 1929, the barn was destroyed by fire. Fortunately, the clock and bell were rescued from the blaze and, ten years later, a group of local residents raised $3,000 to build a tower to hold both items.

The tower was donated to the Town of Bedford, which turned it over to the historical society to maintain. The clock is wound up once a week by a group of volunteer neighbors and continues to strike the hours.

The Bedford Historical Society is based in a building at 612 Old Post Road that had previously served as a country store, post office and an antique shop. Built in 1838, it originally stood on Pound

Ridge Road but was moved to its current site in 1890. The society purchased it in 1968 and, after renovations, it moved its own operation into the building, naming it the Bedford Store.

To learn about other sites in and around the village green, upcoming events and programs or to inquire about museum tours, visit the society or call (914) 234-9751.

Yelverton Inn

In 1721, John Yelverton relocated from New Windsor to Chester, Orange County. Years later, he purchased property where, in 1765, he built an inn. Located on Main Street, the establishment became popular quickly because the main thoroughfare – the King's Highway – ran in front of the establishment. The King's Highway ran from New Windsor to New Jersey. In late 1775 Yelverton passed operations of the inn to his grandson Abijah Yelverton, who managed it through his death in 1832.

Among the parcels of land purchased by the elder Yelverton were three that he earmarked for a "Meeting House or public edifice for the worship of God in any way and manner of those of the Presbyterian persuasion," a parsonage to house its minister, and a graveyard.

In September 1774, a meeting attended by settlers in Goshen and Cornwall was held at the inn to select their first delegate to the Continental Congress in Philadelphia. After the votes were tallied, Henry Wisner was selected, and he left the inn for his journey south. Once there, he protested vehemently against unjust taxation.

During the month of December 1776, troops from Orange and Ulster counties gathered in front of Yelverton's Inn prior to their journey to meet up with Generals Lee and Gates. On Dec. 10, General George Clinton received orders from John McKesson, then secretary of the

Provincial Congress, to "assemble the militia of your brigade as soon as possible in Chester and march them from thence into the state of New Jersey to cooperate with General Lee."

Among the esteemed guests who stayed at the Yelverton Inn during the era was General George Washington, who on July 27, 1782, stopped there on his way from Philadelphia to his Newburgh headquarters at the Hasbrouck house. Three years later, two other notable figures – Alexander Hamilton and Aaron Burr – stayed at the inn while serving as the attorneys of landowners involved in the Wawayanda-Cheesecocks Patent trial, which was held in the Yelverton barn.

The lawsuit was filed because of a boundary dispute between the owners of both patents, due to inexact information in the original drafts. At stake were the titles of many houses already built within both patents.

The two noted politicians would face each other in a duel in Weehawken, New Jersey, on July 11, 1804. At the time Burr was the sitting United States vice president while Hamilton was the former secretary of the treasury. Hamilton was mortally wounded and died.

In 1783, Abijah Yelverton donated one acre of land for church purposes. Fourteen years later, the first meeting house was built and, in 1798, the congregation hired a minister at the cost of $75 per year salary. He also taught school to supplement his earnings.

A portion of the Yelverton Inn was converted into Chester's first library in 1797. Innkeeper Abijah Yelverton became the town's first librarian.

The Yelverton Inn remained under the ownership of the family for six generations. A seventh-generation member of the family was James W. Yelverton, who served as a state senator, representing Schenectady County. In 1869, the inn was sold to the Durland family.

On June 13, 1927, the Minisink Chapter of the Daughters of the American Revolution installed a tablet at the Yelverton Inn in recognition of its history and family oversight for sixty-seven years. The building, now a private residence is located at 112 Main St., Chester.

Take A Day Trip

As was the case in earlier volumes in the Hidden Treasures of the Hudson Valley series, each chapter here includes a physical address so readers can easily visit the sites.

Readers should consider geographically grouping one or more of the fifty-five sites featured here when visiting any one of the counties in the Hudson Valley. Several sites in the more urban parts of Westchester, Orange and parts of Dutchess counties are in close proximity to each other.

Some of the sites are currently used as restaurants, and some also have overnight accommodations, which might make a good home base for overnight or weekend visits. For example, the final home of a signer of the United States Constitution and another private residence that hosted French General Marques de Lafayette during the Revolutionary War are both operating today as bed and breakfast facilities. Similarly, an 18th-century tavern featured in one chapter still serves lunch and dinner to patrons.

Open space is always an important part of community planning in the Hudson Valley, and sites such as Poets' Walk in the Town of Red Hook offer picturesque views of the majestic Hudson River and, in the distance, the Catskill Mountains. Take a stroll along well maintained paths that were once part of the Rokeby estate, now a right of way granted by its current owners.

Visit the only intersection in North America that boasts 18th-century stone buildings on each of its four corners. The district also features the courthouse where African-American civil rights advocate Sojournor Truth successfully petitioned for the return of her son from slavery.

The possibilities for an enlightening and fun-filled day or weekend are endless. Read, learn and embrace the rich history of this historic region in this, the third volume of Hidden Treasures of the Hudson Valley!

Sources

In addition to the invaluable help of those listed on the Acknowledgments page of this book, the author also consulted the following publications.

"Beth David Has Been an Amenia Landmark for 50 Years." Harlem Valley Times. Aug. 21, 1982.

Canning, Jeff and Wally Buxton. History of the Tarrytowns. Harbor Hill Books, 1988.

Caramoor Center for Music and Arts. The Rosen Estate website.

Claverack Centennial Committee. Claverack Township: The History and Heritage. Ideal Printing Company, 1983.

Collard, Edward. Early History of the Fish and Fur Club: The Sesquicentennial Anniversary of Nelsonville. Village Pamphlet, 2005.

"Historic Monroe House's Future Uncertain." Times-Herald Record, April 22, 2017.

Macoubrey, Rev. A.R. The Story of the Old Southeast: Oldest Church in Putnam County.

New York State Office of Parks, Recreation and Historical Preservation Office. Nomination forms.

Pelletreau, William S. History of Putnam County. W.W. Preston Publisher, 1886.

Reynolds, Helen Wilkinson. Dutch Houses of the Hudson Valley Before 1776. Dover Publications, 1965.

Seese, Mildred Parker. Old Orange Houses. Whitlock Press, 1943.

Selsdon, Helen. American Foundation for the Blind. The Gift That Keeps Giving, April 29, 2017.

"Skinny House Big on Family History." Mamaroneck/Larchmont Daily Voice, April 8, 2015.

"Skinny House with Big Aims Vies for Spot in History." New York Times, March 29, 2015.

Stillwaggon, D.A. History of the Township of Shawangunk. D.A. Stillwaggon, Printer, 1955.

The Ferryman. Dobbs Ferry Historical Society. The Story of James Jennings McComb: The Estherwood Connection, Jan. 1995.

Ven. Bhikkhu Bodhi. 50th Anniversary of the Buddhist Association of the U.S., 2014.

William Bull and Sarah Wells Stone House Association website.

About The Author

Anthony Musso is the author of seven previous books:

FDR and the Post Office

Setting the Record Straight: the music and careers of recording artists from the 1950s and 1960s...in their own words, Volume One and Two

Hidden Treasures of the Hudson Valley, Volume One and Two

Staatsburg: A Village Lost In Time

Hidden Treasures of the Catskills

Following a thirty-eight-year career as a writer, editor and media spokesperson for the government, Musso is a weekly columnist and freelance journalist for Gannett Newspapers' Poughkeepsie Journal.

To learn about Anthony Musso's other books or to see a schedule of his speaking engagements, visit www.mussobooks.com.